MW01514600

A Man With A Stick

Against A Man With A

Rock

Mostly Small-Town Baseball Stories

DAVID SAMARAS

ACKNOWLEDGMENTS

Everyone has childhood memories and mine are pretty typical of those of my generation. Transforming these memories into a book became a reality because of the help of two dear friends who are also renowned authors: Marina Osipiva and Ellie Midwood have offered me continuous encouragement, advice, and criticism. There would be no book without the help of these two wonderful people.

My beautiful wife Mary Lee has suffered through hearing me swear at the keyboard and she has shown me, often undeserved, patience and understanding while we tried to figure out how to make the laptop do what I wanted it to do.

To these three wonderful and strikingly beautiful ladies, I offer my humble and sincere;

"Thank You!"

DISCLAIMER

These are my memories and any mistakes, factual or otherwise, are totally of my own making and I take full responsibility for them all.

David Samaras – September 2020.

CONTENTS

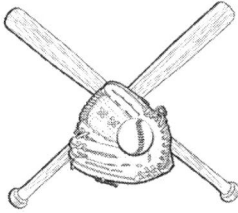

Introduction:

One evening recently, Mary Lee and I were enjoying our twice weekly "Splice the Mainbrace", otherwise known as "bar's-open", at the home of one of our friends. Diane was talking about a book she had been reading in which left-handed pitchers in baseball were described as "flakey", perhaps even crazy. Our friend wanted to know what I thought about that idea. I told her that I was living proof of that statement and was there to tell her that it was true. Every word. I fall into that distinguished category and had my time in the sun as a ballplayer. "Sneaky-fast", is what my opponents called me. I could make my two-seam fastball run away from right-handed batters and I could break a lefty's bat in two with a hard, four-seam fastball, up and in. My curveball would "'drop off the table", leaving hitters shaking their heads as they walked back to the dugout. On the days when I had my "A-Game", I was nearly unhittable. As some of my teammates would say, "I had them eating out of my hands". To be sure, those days were rare but they were real and I remembered them with unabashed pleasure. I fitted the mold of the "flakey-lefty" to a tee.

I was a great one for indulging my baseball superstitions. How?

I talked to myself during games. I respected winning streaks to the point that I tried to make sure nothing changed while one was happening. I didn't want my uniform washed and my routine before a game had to be the same. The unknown cosmic forces that determined the outcomes of games were not to be trifled with. Teammates learned never to talk to me during my pre-game bullpen sessions and to never ask how I am feeling during a game. My focus excluded everyone except my catcher. Him, I trusted above all others. He was an extension of myself. That guy behind the plate, the one I sat next to between innings, he was the one who completed the picture. We got batters out together. We set hitters up for that crucial "out pitch", together. He analyzed my performance like a physicist and a psychiatrist might. Any deviation from the normal routine, he detected and it was immediately brought to my attention. He would stand up and ask the plate umpire for "time", then trot out to the mound. I might get an ass-chewing for losing focus, or I might be told a joke to help me relax and settle down. He might point out a particularly good-looking girl sitting in the stands and say something about her to make me laugh. Then he would plant his gloved hand on my chest and remind me that I could control the outcome of this game and to get my sorry-ass squared away. He would remind me of the current situation, "one out, men on first and second…", and trot back to his position. The pressure was enormous and I loved it. That calls into question my sanity but I always wanted to be the guy with the ball, when the game was on the line.

Sometimes I won. Sometimes I suffered a loss. After all these years, the games seem to coalesce and became less important than they were at the time. What

3

has never dulled is the thrill of the competition. Memories become compressed into moments; when success or failure rested squarely on my shoulders. For us "flakey-left-handers" it always felt like a one-against-one battle. The ancient classic confrontation, the very essence of combat and competition, a guy with a stick against a guy with a rock. It was always intense. It was always personal and I loved it. So, a pleasant conversation at a friend's house, over cocktails, caused me to reminisce on how my love of baseball began and developed through my childhood. What follows is how it happened.

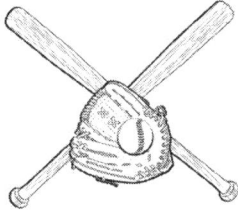

After All These Years

This is a collection of memories and reminiscences, anecdotes, and, silly, pointless stories from a guy who lived in a small town in the Midwest. Living in a small town was boring unless you grew up in one. Those of us who have that experience sometimes look back and think, yeah, I did that, too.

Books usually have plots, a piece of history to be explored and explained, a steamy romance to provide an escape for the reader. This collection has none of these things. No great truths will be discussed, no revelations of great weight are forthcoming. This is not a sophisticated, well-researched and meticulously planned literary work of art. No, this is just a guy telling stories. We are sitting around a table somewhere. Maybe your house or mine. Maybe a quiet bar, or around a crackling firepit on a cool autumn evening. Just a couple of old friends catching up. My stories may jog a memory or two, of some of your own. I hope so. Sit back and laugh, along with me, as we relive some old times.

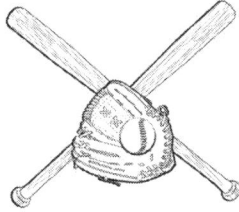

My Greek Heritage – Grandpa Samaras

Grandpa. He was born in a tiny village, in southern Greece, in 1898, the area once known as Sparta and the Spartan blood of heroes flowed in his veins. One of four sons, of Arthur and Pauline Samaras, he came to the United States in 1907, sailing half the length of the Mediterranean, to Gibraltar, then crossing the wide and often angry Atlantic. Back in the days of steam ships, a crossing might take eight weeks to complete. This little, nine-year-old Greek boy spent twice the number of days at sea as did the pilgrims on the Mayflower. It is hard to imagine the conditions aboard those old vessels. There was no first-class accommodations for a poor Greek immigrant. He probably had limited, if any, time on deck,

7

spending his time mostly in the dank and sweltering bowels of a steerage compartment, with little food or fresh water.

Years later, the children of this little Greek immigrant commissioned a plaque, bearing the name of George Arthur Samaras, which hangs on a wall of the Immigration Center on Ellis Island.

Thanks to his uncle and sponsor, George Vriner of Champaign, Illinois, who was the owner of Vriner's Confectionery on Main Street, my Grandpa, my *Papou*, began to learn the restaurant business. His dream gradually evolved into the desire to become a candy maker.

His apprenticeship was slow. He started at the bottom, as a dish washer in the back of the restaurant. Later, as he began to speak and understand the new language, he waited tables but he wanted to learn how to make candy! In order to realize his dream, he once again had to start at the bottom. He carried the candy-making supplies into the store. Heavy burlap bags, filled with raw peanuts; 50lb blocks of chocolate, wrapped in heavy, waxed paper; bags of sugar; pecans; barrels of corn syrup, and a myriad of other ingredients. As he worked, he watched and learned. He helped in making candy canes, a Vriner's specialty. A sugar and water mix was heated to 400 degrees, stirred, and then poured onto a marble cooling table. As the mixture cooled, it thickened and became pliable. A portion is sliced off and a mixture of red and blue dye is blended together and squeezed in long stripes. The amber-colored sugar syrup turns white as it cools and is rolled into a thick log. Next, the band of red and blue stripes, which has become a burgundy color, is wrapped around the white sugar log. The log is stretched and twisted to the desired thickness and individual candy canes are snipped off. The process required coordination and strength. Pulling and twisting warm strands of candy was something everyone working in the restaurant helped with and my grandpa soon became quite competent.

From that introduction to the art of making candy, he slowly but steadily progressed. He learned how to make English Toffee, maple and vanilla cream centers and he learned how to prepare the chocolate for dipping creams, peanut clusters, turtles, and a dozen more varieties of candy. Vriner's became well-known all over the State, for their fine candies and especially the candy canes. His uncle's English Toffee recipe was sold to a man named Heath who made candy bars. The years passed and young George grew into a hardworking, confident, young man.

By 1917, my grandpa had still not yet earned his U.S. citizenship but he enlisted in the army, when his adopted country went to war with Germany. After training in South Carolina, Pvt. Samaras was assigned to the 53rd. Pioneer Regiment. He and the rest of his unit boarded the USS Mongolia and set sail for France. Twelve days later they shuffled down the gangplank in Brest and three days after that, they were at the front.

The twenty-year-old, Greek immigrant fought in two major battles in France, the St. Michel offensive and the Meuse Argonne offensive. He was wounded in the Argonne forest. Out of his 75-man unit, my Grandpa was one of only seven survivors of a brutal artillery barrage. He never said much to me about what he did during the war but his medals indicated that he had fought in two major battles. He did tell me that he had been wounded in his legs and that from time to time, he could pluck tiny slivers of German steel from them. He carried shrapnel in his legs for the rest of his life.

In 1920, George Samaras married Edna Hullinger and on June 29, 1921, in Champaign, Illinois, (or nine months later) their first-born son, my dad, Alexander George was born. Edna, my Grammy Samaras, was a tall, sturdy woman with intense blue eyes. I don't know much about her younger life except for this small tidbit. She had a sister named Leota who was a professional dancer. She married a man named Joe Yule who was an actor. Their son, Joe Yule Jr., became an actor and went by the stage name of Mickey Rooney. I remember grammy as always being behind the cash-register at the Ritz in Hoopeston. I think she must have insisted that her home be an "English-speaking-only" home because neither she, nor any of her children, learned to speak Greek. She doted on her grandchildren, me especially and boy could she cook and bake!

The George Samaras family lived in Champaign until Alexy was in grade school. One of his favorite past-times was to build model airplanes out of balsawood, then climb on the roof of their house on South Neil Street, set the tail of the plane on fire, and sail it through the air. That might explain some of the stupid stuff his oldest son would do in the years to come.

Grandpa was ready to strike out on his own in the restaurant and candy-making business. He bought a restaurant in Hoopeston, Illinois and made his home there. The Ritz Confectionery and Restaurant, located in the middle of Main Street, right across the street from Murphy's Dime Store became a very successful enterprise. Grandpa modelled it after the interior of Vriner's. At the entrance, there was a long candy case on one side and an eight-stool soda fountain on the right. Further back were the booths and tables. The kitchen and the candy-making area was in the very back of the store. When we moved to Hoopeston in 1950, my dad went into partnership with my Grandpa and they ran the restaurant together for 10 years.

My favorite areas were the soda fountain and the candy making area. I learned how to make ice-cream sodas, parfaits, shakes, and malts. With a variety of flavored and colored syrups ready to be pumped into a glass, I learned to make "green-rivers, vanilla and cherry cokes, banana-splits", and sundaes of all kinds. The best part was spending time watching grandpa make his candy. There was a long marble table, maybe eight-feet by four-feet, a heated vat filled with warm, viscous chocolate, a copper kettle three-feet in diameter and two-feet deep that sat on a cast-iron gas burner. This is where he roasted the raw peanuts. That heavenly aroma has stayed with me but to accurately describe it is beyond my poor, literary powers. He stirred the peanuts into hot oil with what looked like a shortened boat oar. Slowly and with the tenderness of a lover, he pushed and pulled that oar through the golden mass. Often, he worked into the night, especially before the big candy holidays of Christmas, Valentine's Day, and Easter.

Our family would come back to the store, after supper, to watch him work. There was a huge, wooden Philco radio, with a dimly lit area, displaying a variety of wavelengths, including short-wave. I remember listening to the old radio version of "Gun-Smoke" narrated by William Conrad. The big marble table was where he poured and cooled his English toffee, peanut brittle, maple and vanilla creams, and nougat. With the creams, once they cooled, he cut them into long strips and pinched them off into bite-sized portions. He then rolled them in his hands and set them near the vat of chocolate. He showed me how to dip the creams in chocolate and set them aside on the wax-paper covered, cooling racks. The thick, liquid chocolate was warm, not hot and held to an exact temperature, for reasons known only to grandpa. It was true art. Each piece was finished with a tiny, curly Q on top and continued to glisten even after it cooled. He also molded solid pieces of chocolate into different shapes. Santa's reindeer and gingerbread men for Christmas, chocolate hearts for Valentine's Day, and bunnies, eggs, and an ornate chocolate church for Easter.

Grandpa made candy every day to keep up with the demand. Anyone walking by his area would see him, with a huge smile on his face and chocolate up to his elbows, as he dipped vanilla creams, maple creams, peanut clusters, nougat, English toffee nougats and turtles.

The Ritz was always busy at lunch time. Customers came and went through the front door, as well as through the back door. People leaving through the back door, after lunch, customarily helped themselves to a piece of candy from one of the cooling racks as they passed by. Just the normal thing to do at the Ritz.

My grandpa was small in stature, maybe five-feet-two-inches tall but he had a broad chest and massive forearms. He was always a bundle of happy energy. He never learned to drive a car and so walked to and from work every day. He had a wonderful and mischievous sense of humor and a few decidedly and sometimes, slightly off-putting, Greek idiosyncrasies. He loved to eat raw garlic. "Is good for you!" he would always say.

I will always remember the time we took him to the Lorraine Theater to see some movie we thought he would like. The place was crowded, nearly every seat filled. The smell of garlic hung in the air and there came a point, maybe halfway through the movie, when we noticed that all the seats in front of us, behind us and on both sides, were vacant. We had become an island in the middle of the theater. We laughed about that for a long time after.

His sense of humor came to the fore on April Fool's Day year after year. The people who were in the habit of grabbing a piece of candy on their way to the back door, after lunch, got a surprise. Some of the peanut clusters were substituted with navy beans, the creams were laced with Tabasco sauce, an English toffee became a chocolate covered bar of hotel soap. Year after year, it worked every time. It worked so well that I decided to try it.

I never locked my locker at school and there was usually a sack filled with my grandpa's candy inside for me and my friends to enjoy. One April Fool's Day, the candy was a little different and it cost me a girlfriend. She liked to hang around my locker between classes, demurely nibbling on exquisite chocolates. On this particular day, her eyes got as big as saucers, her face got red, and she raced to the nearest drinking fountain. Of course, I was doubled over laughing but for some reason she was not so amused. Her ponytail kept perfect time with her shoes, banging on the tile floor, as she stormed off.

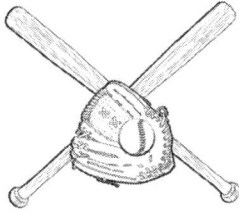

The Man Who Taught Me To Play Baseball

As I have already mentioned, my dad, Alexander George Samaras, was born in 1921. Young Alexy began taking piano lessons at age nine and it was clear, to Mrs. Blankenship, his teacher, that the boy had talent. Lots of talent but music wasn't little Alexy's only passion. In 1933, he had an opportunity to attend the World's Fair in Chicago. Along with several of his grade-school classmates, he boarded an Illinois-Central, Pullman car, at the depot in his hometown of Hoopeston and chugged north under a billowing cloud of black, coal smoke. The soothing, rhythmic clack of steel wheels on steel tracks, much like the metronome, which ruled his life at the piano, relaxed him, as he formulated his plan.

The group of students were allowed to roam the grounds of the massive Expo unescorted but they were instructed to meet, at a location near Grant Park, at 6:00pm. Alexy had his window of opportunity! Instead of touring the exhibitions and gorging on strange and exotic foods, he walked a few short blocks to State Street and boarded the northbound 'EL' train and for a mere twenty cents, rode to the Addison Street stop. This was to be his World's Fair! Wrigley Field! A dollar and ten cents bought him a grandstand ticket to the baseball cathedral of his dreams. All afternoon he watched the God-like figures of Gabby Hartnett, Billy Herman, Kiki Cuyler, Stan Hack, Charlie Grimm, and the rest of his Cub heroes play baseball. The center of his universe was located at the corner of Addison and Clark Streets in Chicago and for the first time in his life he was part of it.

After the game, he joined the throng of happy Cubs fans on the southbound 'EL' train and made his rendezvous at Grant Park with time to spare. A lifelong love affair with the often hapless, but always exciting, Chicago Cubs had begun and 20 years later, he passed that love affair along to his first-born son. Me!

My dad graduated from high school in 1939. He studied music at Illinois State Normal University in Bloomington and somewhere between playing Varsity Tennis and piano, he met Carolyn Jean Brown.

Carolyn was a cute, little, brown-eyed farm girl, from the tiny town of Divernon, Illinois. I don't think I ever knew what she studied in college, only that she dropped out after her second year, in 1943, when her husband went to war. As my mom, I am sure that there were many times when she felt overwhelmed. My brothers and I were a handful. I remember once, after a football game at Illinois, I was walking across the field when a young man close to my age came up to me and said, "you may not remember me. I am John Stuebe. We lived on Maple Street in Hoopeston." Sure, I remembered. We used to play together and get into trouble together a lot. Later, when I told mom about the meeting, she said, "oh yes, not that long ago John's mother called to chat and reminded me that when the kids were little, she told John to stay off Lincoln Street because those Samaras boys are just too rough." So, yeah. My mom had a tough time keeping us in line. The words, "just wait till your father gets home!" still have a familiar ring. Our house was always neat and clean, despite our efforts to reduce it to rubble. She tended to numerous cuts and bruises and was in a constant state of worry over the health and safety of her children. My brothers and I were far luckier than we realized, to have her for a mom.

Dad was in the ROTC (Reserve Officers Training Corps) program there and chose to be in the cavalry. There was a lot of leather to be polished and lots of horse manure to be cleaned out of the stables.

In 1943, he graduated and almost immediately enrolled in the V-12 Program, the Navy Midshipman training, to become a Naval Officer. Three months later, he was commissioned an Ensign in the US Naval Reserve, in a ceremony at Northwestern University, in Evanston, Illinois.

On December 26, 1943, he and Carolyn were married and after a fleeting honeymoon, he was off to war. During the nearly three years the newlyweds were apart, Carolyn left college and worked at the YMCA to earn money for the household she dreamed of. She saved every penny and when she had enough, she bought a piano for her husband. What a sweet surprise it was for him, when he returned home after the war! Yet, before that would happen, Ensign Samaras continued his training in Amphibious Warfare, at the Naval Base in Little Creek VA. By March 1944, he was the skipper of LCT 709, a flat bottomed, 152-foot-long ship capable of carrying 250-tons of men and equipment onto a beach. Later, in his stories about the war, dad always referred to it as a part of the "Bathtub Navy". His little ship rode piggyback on a much larger LST to cross the Atlantic, in the early spring of 1944. He was part of a 70-ship convoy, sailing at a sluggish 10-knots, through U-boat infested waters. Deck watch lookouts were rotated every 30 minutes because of the bitter cold and wet conditions.

While on watch one night, Ensign Samaras saw a tanker blow up just 1,000 yards away. The sea lit up all around and he could see the torpedo wake tracking straight toward him. The hold of the LST, carrying his little LCT, was loaded to the gills with ammunition. The torpedo struck the hull of the LST and did not explode. Years later, Dad told me that was the instant he became a fatalist.

Once in England, he had time to visit London. He

was in Trafalgar Square, just minutes before a V1 buzz-bomb exploded. There, he met another man from his hometown of Hoopeston, Illinois. Ken Hammond was a U.S. Army doctor and much later, after the war, he became our family physician.

LCT709 was moored in Plymouth, England. On the evening of June 4, 1944, his little ship slipped its moorings. LCT709 set sail for Normandy, across the gray and wind-swept English Channel, as part of the huge invasion armada. Halfway across the Channel, they were ordered to return to Plymouth. The invasion had been postponed for 24-hours in the hope that there would be an improvement in the foul weather.

On June 6, 1944, Ensign Samaras ran his little LCT up onto Utah Beach. An LCT is designed to run toward a beach at full speed, about 8 knots. Several yards offshore, the crew drops an anchor, which is attached to a long cable, then they run the ship aground on the beach. To pull off the beach, a winch winds the cable and the ship backs off the beach.

Under sporadic and sometimes heavy, machine-gun and mortar fire, Ensign Samaras discharged his cargo of soldiers of the Fourth Infantry Division, along with trucks, tanks, and jeeps but was unable to pull off the beach because the anchor cable, attached to the winch, had become fouled in the ship's screws. For seven hours, crew members, including the Skipper, took turns going over the side with a hack-saw in a desperate attempt to cut the cable. Finally freed, they were able to drift, with the tide, to deeper water.

Day after day, week after week, LCT709 unloaded men and equipment and brought casualties back. Finally, harbors were secured and repaired and the job of the Bathtub Navy, in Normandy, was finished.

Ensign Samaras packed his sea bag and his sea chest and returned home for 30-days leave. After being promoted to LT(jg), he rode a train across the country to the West Coast. LT(jg) Samaras was assigned XO (Executive Officer) on the LCS(L) 81.

Landing Craft Support (Large) is a seaworthy vessel with a range of 5,500 nautical miles. Just 158-feet in length, those little ships bristled with anti-aircraft guns. Twin, mounted, 40mm Bofors Anti-aircraft guns fore and aft, 20 mm Anti-aircraft guns all around, and a slew of

.50cal. machine guns. They set a course of two-seven-zero, out of San Francisco and sailed west, across the vast Pacific.

At Pearl Harbor, they refueled and provisioned, then headed into enemy waters, bound for Okinawa. Once in the anchorage offshore from the embattled island, 81 was assigned to Flotilla Four (The Mighty Midgets). Their task was radar-picket-duty and shooting down Kamikazes in a sector northwest of Okinawa. The crew stood at battle-stations for 77 consecutive days. They were attacked by Japanese suicide planes, shooting down three of them and the Flotilla boasted of; "the Highest Score in Naval Anti-aircraft History".

When the war ended, my dad was on Occupation Duty in Japan, while his beloved Cubs played in their first World Series since 1908.

When he returned home, the new G.I. Bill allowed him to study at Julliard and to earn his Master's Degree from Columbia University in New York. He and my mom lived in Harlem, at 103rd Street and 3rd Avenue. Had I been just a couple of weeks premature, I would have been born a New Yorker but I didn't arrive until January

1947.

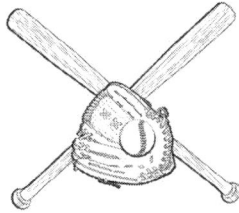

My Hometown

At the end of 1950, my parents moved to Hoopeston, Illinois, a small town of about 6,500; home to several agricultural industries, two canning factories, "Joan of Arc Company", "Stokely", the "Farm Machinery Corporation", and the "American Can Company".

My home for almost 10 years, from age-three to age-twelve, was at 846 East Lincoln Street. We were the third house from the end of the block and, for a long time, from the end of the town. East Lincoln Street was made of brick, probably the result of a Depression-Era project, slick and shiny when it rained. Car traffic made a soft rumbling sound when the tires hit the bricks. Beautiful Maple and Elm trees formed a flowing, sparkling canopy. Our house was white-stucco, with the trim painted forest-

27

green. We used to place our empty half-gallon milk jugs on the front steps and the milkman replaced them with full ones, three times a week. Our big, side-yard, butted up against Mr. Nelson's hedge (sometimes referred to as the left-field foul line). The yard served as a football field, a baseball field, a place to make giant leaf piles, and a place to learn the joy of pushing an old-fashioned lawn-mower, in straight lines, without missing a spot.

I still remember our phone number was 1129. A heavy, black, bakelite telephone, sat on a cabinet in the dining room. To make a call, all we had to do was pick up the receiver and wait for the operator to say, "number please". Our mailman, Delmer, visited twice a day with letters, bills, and magazines. My mom looked forward to her issues of "Look", "Life", "Collier's", and "The Saturday Evening Post". My dad got his "Sports Illustrated" and I got "Boys Life" magazine.

The driveway ran between the house and the big side yard. Halfway up the driveway was the carport. It was a fancy, pillared affair, with a flat roof, which became a collection point for errant footballs, baseballs, basketballs, and whiffle balls. My brother Paul was two years younger.

When we weren't fighting, we were best buddies. We could climb out a second-story bathroom window and retrieve them. We could also use that roof as the perfect place to assault unwary passersby, with snowballs, in the winter. Further back, the garage featured a basketball hoop and net, and inside was the usual junk, including two old saw-horses, with saddles on them. Paul and I spent countless hours astride these saddles, being "The Lone Ranger", "Gene Autry", maybe "Hopalong Cassidy", or any number of cowboy heroes we had seen at the Saturday Matinee at the Lorraine Theater downtown.

The back yard had a grape arbor and my mom and grandmommy Brown made grape jelly right up until the year that my brother and I discovered that hard, green, unripe grapes made excellent slingshot ammo. The white, peeling, wooden fence along the back had a peach basket nailed to it. It was a perfect place to grow up, for a young boy.

When I was a baby, my mother was frantic. She thought that there must be something wrong with me, because I couldn't feed myself. That is, until she put the spoon in my left hand. After that, she probably still thought I was retarded but for a number of different reasons. From the time I could walk, I took great delight in throwing things. When I was old enough to play outside (a time that could not come soon enough to suit my mother), I threw anything I could wrap my usually dirty, little hands around.

One of my favorite targets was Mr. Erickson's trash can. I stood in the alley behind our house and threw rocks at the bright, silver can. I could ping that can with increasing regularity. Finally, Mrs. Erickson called my mom, "Carolyn, can you please make that kid stop? He is driving me crazy over here." Okay, it was time to find a new target. Throwing mud balls at the white stucco side of our garage seemed like a good idea and it was, right up until my dad came home. That evening, I exercised my arm with a scrub brush and a bucket of water. I scoured that wall until I was sure it was clean. Dad came out to inspect my work. I refilled the bucket and scrubbed until I was sure I would drop dead. Three inspections later, I was sent to the basement to take off my muddy clothes. A bath, where more scrubbing was inflicted on me, then supper.

My dad came up with a solution the next day. He

came home early, with a peach basket and a dozen baseballs. He stepped off a distance away from the fence and drew a line in the dirt. Next, he nailed the basket to the fence. That was the beginning of my baseball education and the first spark of the intense love for the game that I carry to this day.

We started going to Cub games at Wrigley Field, when I was three. The drive took just over an hour. Green and brown farm fields and small towns gradually turned into concrete and tall shiny buildings. My face pressed to the window, my fingers drumming with nervous excitement, we drove up Route 1, through Kankakee then Chicago Heights. North on Stoney Island to 95th Street. Left on 95th to Halstead. North to Belmont Avenue, then right on Sheffield. Green and white elevated trains raced by, screeching on quivering rails. My widening eyes peered through the fog my breath created on the car window.

I still can see, in my mental eye, the stadium rising above the neighborhood. A magnificent edifice of gray and green, brightly colored flags, on the rooftop, fluttering in the breeze. This was the place where dreams were made.

We drove up and down crowded northside streets looking for a place to park. Finally, an open space.

For the first couple of years, I didn't get much out of those trips to Chicago but I could see the excitement, the joy, and the intensity, in my dad's eyes as I watched him follow the game. Eventually, after listening to Jack Quinlan and Lou Boudreau broadcasting the games on WGN radio in Chicago, day after day, all spring and summer, I started to visualize the action and to understand how the game was played. Trips to the ballpark became more memorable, more exciting. We handed our tickets to the Andy Frain usher and pushed through the turnstile. Dad would buy two scorecards and two pencils. The concourse was noisy, dimly lit, and crowded with fans. Food vendors were everywhere, selling hot dogs, beer, peanuts. Guys selling caps and tee-shirts scurried among the onlookers. We walked up the concrete steps and I remember audibly gasping at the sight. Bright sunshine. The beautiful green grass, the curved symmetry of the infield, the ivy-covered outfield wall. It took my breath away the first time I saw it and it still does.

We always tried to arrive early enough to watch

batting practice. A wooden bat making contact with a snow-white baseball sounded like a gunshot. Long, line-drives soar into the outfield. Occasionally, someone would hit a majestic fly-ball that carried over the wall, into the bleachers, where fans scrambled to grab a precious souvenir. Add to all of this excitement, the taste of salted peanuts in the shell, a hot-dog with mustard, and a frosty-malt, in a paper cup, with a little wooden spoon. A perfect day! I was hooked; a brand-new Cub fan for life.

Baseball was what most of the boys did in Hoopeston, from the first warm day of spring until right before Halloween; after school until supper time and when school let out for the summer vacation, we played from morning until it was too dark to see. All day, every day.

We looked for empty lots we could convert into ballfields. A flat rock might be home plate, maybe some old burlap bags for bases, and we were all set. Broken bats, held together with sticky, black tape, baseballs scuffed and often a little lopsided, were the tools of our trade.

Sometimes, the rules of the game had to be altered, depending on the layout of the field and the number of guys who showed up to play that day. If we didn't have enough for a real game, we made up games. "Flies and Grounders to 500", "Pepper", "Pitcher's Hand Out", "Right or Left Field Closed". I am sure you remember them all and are smiling, just like I am, right now. Sometimes we were smart enough to bring our own lunch but usually guys took off, to get home and grab a quick baloney or peanut-butter and jelly sandwich and to gulp down a glass of milk just before moms' heard back doors slam all over the neighborhood.

When I was old enough to start playing Little-League baseball, the intensity of my workouts, with dad, continued to increase. He would drum into my head, "walks will kill you. Every time you walk a batter, you better believe he is going to score." I pitched and pitched and pitched to him, when he got home from work. The "twenty-strikes-in-a-row" rule was hard and fast. Before I could ride my bike out to McFarren Park to the city pool, I had to throw 20-strikes-in-a-row and then I could go. There were many days that I stood in the front yard facing my dad, with tears in my eyes, struggling to throw strikes.

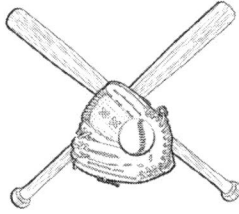

Pickup Games

My glove hooked to the handlebars of my bike, my bat slung over my shoulder, a baseball rolling back and forth in the basket, I was on my way to McFarren Park. I had no plans other than to play baseball with whoever would show up. This was my element and always much more fun than the organized Little-League games, with coaches. Sometimes, there was no one else around when I skidded my bike to a dusty halt behind the backstop. It didn't matter. I threw the ball up and hit it into the screen, for a while.

As though it happened just yesterday, I can still hear the sound of a white-ash baseball bat making contact with a white, horsehide baseball. It was music to my ears. I would visualize myself in Wrigley Field, drilling an inside fastball deep into the bleachers in right center. The crowd roars as I trot around the bases. A handshake from the third-base coach and a moment later, I leap into the arms of the reception committee waiting for me at home plate.

Okay, time to loosen up. I step off the distance and start throwing the ball into the screen of the backstop. My windup is a combination of Sandy Koufax and Warren Spahn, my two leftie Major League heroes. My arms swing back, then up over my head, my left foot pivots against the pitching rubber, followed by a high, graceful leg-kick and the foot hits the ground in a perfect line with home plate. My hips and shoulders torque, which transfers all the power I have generated to my left arm. It snaps through the air, like a whip, as the ball leaves my hand. Fastball! Strike One!

Some kids who are riding around the park, on their bikes, pull up and head for the field. Others race home to get their gloves and bats. Game on! Even if there are only two of us, we find ways to have fun. Playing catch and chatting, taking turns hitting fly balls and grounders to each other, or just talking about our favorite players.

Soon, there are more bikes barreling into the ballpark area. Big kids, little kids, some guys I know from school or Little-League, and sometimes guys I have never met. With a cap on your head and a leather glove on your hand, you became a brother, a teammate, and a rival.

We all play and laugh together, bound by our love for the game. Four or five of us could play a game of "Pepper". One guy hits groundballs to the others lined up across from him. Field the ball and begin flipping it from one glove to the next down the line, with the last guy tossing it toward the hitter. Catch a line drive or a pop and you get to have a bat. Muff a groundball or miss a flip and you go to the end of the line. If the batter swings and misses, he grabs his glove and goes to the end of the line and the first one in the line gets to bat. If there are more of us but not quite enough to start a real game, we play, "500". One guy throws the ball up and hits flies and grounders to the rest of us scattered all around the field. Catch a flyball and you get 100 points. Cleanly field a ground ball and it's 50 points. Miss a fly or muff a grounder and you lose the points. The first one to get to 500, gets to bat. When enough people finally show up, we choose up sides. Two captains are selected, usually the two oldest guys, or the first ones to get to the field that day. Somebody tosses one of the captains a bat. He grabs it down by the barrel. The two captains then go, "Knob Up", grabbing the bat and going hand over hand until one of the captains touches the knob. He gets to pick first and they choose up sides for the game.

The little kids usually get picked last and end up playing right field. I guess it amounts to a kind of, "rite-of-passage". The game starts and we play. Inning after inning, great plays, headfirst slides, errors, disputed calls, sizzling line drives, getting hit by pitches. No walks were allowed, you had to hit the ball.

There was lots of joking and kidding around to accompany our intense competition and I don't remember a single fight among the kids in all those many games. We always made sure the little kids got to hit the ball and run the bases. At first, we'd try to keep score but after a few innings, the score didn't matter anymore. All we cared about was, "how many outs" and "who's up next". The better players helped the younger, less experienced ones. Any time I saw a player who I thought might be better than

I was, I always tried to learn what he was doing and copy him.

We competed and we tried hard to win but most of the competition was with ourselves. We all shared the same dream and we knew we had to keep getting better. Time stands still, as it always does when we play baseball. Guys take off and go home for some lunch or a snack. More guys show up and get assigned to a team and so on it goes, throughout the day.

Occasionally a mom will drive up and tell some kid it was time to come home and there were even a few times when moms would show up with a big pitcher of Kool-Aid, paper cups, and cookies. The game goes on until it gets too dark to see. If we had been able to figure out how to turn on the lights, we would have played until our parents dragged us off the field.

I was back aboard my bike and headed home. I was dirty, sweaty, happy, maybe a little tired but already getting excited about tomorrow's game.

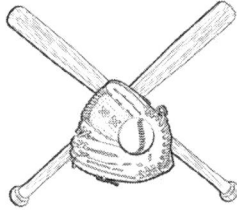

Some of the Other Things Small-Town Boys Did to Have Fun

Of course, my friends and I couldn't play baseball all the time but when rain, snow, cold-weather, being chased out of an empty-lot by a construction crew, or darkness made us find other activities to stay busy and out of the house, we played marbles. Little, glass balls about one half-inch in diameter, most of them were called cat's-eyes because of the little colored sliver embedded in each marble. Others were solid colors but the best ones, the most prized and sought after were the "steelies". These were steel ball-bearings someone's dad brought home from the plant or machine shop. Sometimes we found them on the ground. The big ones, maybe an inch or more in diameter, "shooters". Some were big cat's-eyes, but the best ones were always the steelies.

My dad showed me how he used to play marbles when he was a kid. They drew a three-foot circle in the dirt and they shot at each other's marbles by flicking them with their thumbs.

We had our own rules. Our games covered more distance. We would stand and throw our shooters at an opponent's marbles. When we hit one, it was ours and it went into our marble bags. We played during recesses at school or while walking home after school. Everyone had a marble bag. Most were cloth bags with a drawstring. Mine was soft brown-leather and it bulged with my winnings. I liked to heft it in my hands, imagining that it was filled with gold coins or nuggets; the muffled clinking sound of all that loot was like music.

Our marble bags were our American Express Cards. We never left home without them. We bought our marbles at Murphy's Dime Store. Why stores like Murphy's were called dime-stores was a mystery to me but that's what our parents called them. Good enough for me.

Murphy's had everything! My mom bought lots of

things there; stationery, stockings, stuff for the kitchen, bars of soap. One side of the store was all toys and stuff for hobbies. Sticks of almost weightless balsa wood for making model airplanes, glue, little jars of paint, brushes, plastic model kits for making airplanes, ships, tanks, race cars, and other neat stuff. Some of it was girl stuff like paper dolls, real dolls, yarn – weird stuff like that. The rest of the store was the good stuff. Cowboy hats, gun and holster sets, bow and arrows, dart guns, squirt guns, cap guns, bean shooters, sling shots, plastic army men, baseballs, footballs, baseball cards. Everything. It was all there at Murphy's.

Wide-eyed little boys and girls tugging at mom's sleeve and whining, "I need one of those; Keith has one just like it. Can I have this one? Aw mom, please…". The excitement was never-ending and sometimes I got lucky to bring home something special.

After supper, during the summer, the kids in the neighborhood played "Kick the Can". Kind of like Hide and Seek. If you could get back and kick the can before somebody tagged you, then you were home safe. Something like that. The rules weren't too important but running around, hiding, laughing, and sneaking up on people, that is what kept us busy.

Most of these games took place on Washington Street, one street over from Maple, where most of the other kids lived. The Anderson's lived in a big house with a big front porch. There were three daughters, Lucia, Helen, and Peggy. Lucia was a couple of years older than the rest of us. She was getting tired of all our "kid" games but she had the task of looking after her younger sisters. Helen was my age and I thought of her as, "one of the guys".

Peggy was different. She *was* one of the guys, only prettier. A lot prettier. There was something about her, I guess, something inexplicable. I didn't start to figure it all out until I was in Junior-High. Of all the sisters, she was my favorite. Long blond, braided pigtails, mesmerizing huge blue eyes, and long tanned legs. She was nice and so cute that I always found it kind of hard to talk to her. We spent a lot of time sitting on that big front porch. Mrs. Anderson would bring out cookies and milk for all of us but what I remember about her most was that she could throw, catch, spit, run, and get dirty with the best of us. Only this chain of consciousness made me think about her but she is probably the reason that I have always considered myself a "leg man". Who knows?

I think most of my friends were sons of World-War-Two veterans. Sometimes a guy would bring out something he found in the attic, or the basement, to show the rest of us. It might be a German helmet or a belt-buckle, a Jap flag, a bayonet. Our dads were heroes in our eyes and the stories about them and the things they occasionally told us were amazing.

My friends and I played "Army" a lot. We put on helmets that were way too big and heavy for us and we crawled around in the dirt, hiding under bushes, all over the neighborhood. We killed millions of Japs and Germans. When one of the guys came out with a string of firecrackers, we discovered explosives. Now, we're talking!

Lots of people who lived in Hoopeston came from Kentucky where selling fireworks was legal. We started to get our hands on M80's, cherry-bombs, bottle-rockets, and those little strings of firecrackers. Blowing stuff up and generating a lot of noise became our passion.

The cherry-bomb was the ultimate weapon. A red

ball, a little smaller than a ping-pong ball, with a green, waxed fuse, it would even explode underwater. A roadside mailbox would almost disappear if someone tossed a cherry-bomb inside. One time, somebody dropped one into a toilet at school. Instant day off for everybody, while a plumber repaired the damage. Something this much fun to do just naturally has to escalate. My brother and I decided to try to make some gunpowder. Hey, it seemed like a good idea at the time.

We bought sulfur and saltpeter from the drugstore (for a science experiment, we said), crushed some charcoal briquettes with a hammer, for the carbon we needed and messed around with different proportions, with no luck. Somehow, one of our mixtures got wet. When it dried out, we touched a match to a small pinch of it. A rapid fizz, some sparks, and a lot of acrid smoke. Oh yeah! We were about to conquer the world! We packed the mixture into a wooden matchbox, then tried to make a fuse. By this time, our laboratory had moved to my brother's bedroom. That was just one of the bad decisions we made that day.

The next one was to roll a strip of the gunpowder into a piece of notebook paper. I tested the fuse.

Unfortunately, the other end was too close to the match box. There was no explosion, but there was a huge amount of fizzing and lots, and I mean it, lots of billowing, black, choking smoke. Mom came running up the stairs and flung open the door.

We looked up in shock and horror to see her stagger away from the open door. The ensuing phone call to our dad indicated that she was not amused.

We feared a punishment from our dad and waited for him on the front porch. First, he checked us over and since we were unhurt, at least not as of yet, he went upstairs to my brother's room, which was coated in soot from floor to ceiling. My dad came back to the porch and announced that Paul would be moving into my room for a while. Then he ordered us to the car.

To add to our terror, he spoke no harsh words to us as we pulled out of the driveway. We drove to the edge of town, then out into the countryside, almost to the Indiana border. It seemed like a long way. Suddenly, he stopped at the side of a country road and ordered us out of the car. We stood there while he got back into the car and backed around, until it was facing back toward town. He said, "I am extremely disappointed in you two boys. I have never seen your mother so hysterical as she was today. You scared her to death. Here's what is going to happen. You are both going to run in front of the car all the way home. Don't you dare stop!" He got back into the car and leaned his head out the window. "Get moving!" We ran and we ran and we ran some more.

The lights of town gradually got bigger, closer. We reached the city limits and turned onto our street. When we climbed onto the porch, he yelled, "wait there!" After he put the car away in the garage, he came to us and said, "the first thing you are going to do is apologize to your mother. Then, you will take your showers and go to bed. Your school's track season starts tomorrow and you are both going out for the team. We already know you can run."

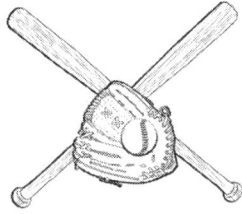

Camping Out

I was probably six or seven when I joined the Cub Scouts. I don't know why exactly. Probably because some of my pals had joined and their moms called my mom. Who knows? It was really kind of boring. There were meetings at someone's house. That mom was the "Den Mother" because we were supposed to be a pack of cubs. The best part was the little uniforms we wore, blue shirts with various patches sewn on the sleeves and the yellow neckerchief. The caps were dumb looking little beanies with short bills but the rest of the uniform looked like the ones the cavalry soldiers wore in the westerns we watched every Saturday afternoon at the Lorraine Theater.

At the meetings, we did little crafts like making

bracelets or potholders, boring stuff like that. I stuck it out until I was old enough to become a Boy-Scout. Boy-Scouts! That was a lot more fun. During the winter, there were meetings, usually in some church basement. We studied different parts of the "Boy-Scout Handbook" and had to learn the Boy-Scout Oath to recite it at the beginning and at the end of the meetings. We performed different interesting tasks in order to earn round "merit badges" which we had sewn on our greenish-brown uniforms. I earned a few merit badges but the real reason I wanted to be a Boy-Scout was because they got to go on camping trips.

My first night in a tent, my first time away from home except for overnights with my grandparents, was memorable. I had a flimsy, cotton, sleeping-bag and slept on the ground in a leaky tent. Oh yes, it rained! Check that. It poured! Our Scout Leader forgot to tell us about digging a trench around our tents to siphon away rainwater. Everything was soaked and muddy. I'll admit that I didn't have much fun that night and I'm pretty sure that the parents who were called, in the middle of the night, to come out and pick up their kids, weren't having much fun either. I guess you could say that the whole thing was a complete washout. Was I discouraged from going on more campouts? No way. I couldn't wait to get back out into the woods.

My parents bought all the necessary Boy-Scout gear; a ruck sack, a canteen and mess kit, a better sleeping bag, uniforms, and a hunting knife. I was ready!

There was a Boy-Scout camp at a place called Portland Arch, somewhere in Indiana. It became my home-away-from-home for a couple of weeks during the late Summer and early Fall, for a few years. The outings lasted one week but I usually went for two. We cooked over open fires in the evenings. My favorite 'dish' was ground beef, chopped up potatoes and onions. We wrapped this combination in tin-foil and tossed it into the fire. After a half-hour or so, we would poke the wrap out of the fire and drop it onto the plate of the mess kit. Prying the foil away with a fork, we would inhale the exquisite aroma and partake of some fine dining, Boy-Scout style.

We looked for hollow reeds and tried our hand at smoking and sometimes we actually produced smoke. Hot stuff and we knew it. We often went on hikes in the woods, paddled canoes around a lake, and went swimming. In the quiet moments, we whittled on pieces of wood with our official Boy-Scout pocketknives. We learned techniques for tracking each other through the woods.

Portland Arch was a huge area and Scouts from all over Illinois and Indiana gathered there. Naturally, there arose some conflicts. Artificially manufactured rivalries to be sure but probably the normal reaction of young boys away from home and possibly, experiencing the first effects of testosterone. In other words, we had fights.

I became friends with a kid from Vincennes, Indiana. He fancied himself a tough guy and after the requisite, pushing, shoving, challenging, and fisticuffs, we became inseparable. We roamed campsites looking for fights. I guess we were trying to prove ourselves, maybe trying to impress each other with our fighting spirit. Testing our limits. But we weren't bullies. We never picked on younger guys, or anyone who didn't share our newfound interests. No, we went after the older, bigger guys, the camp counselors, just to see if we could face them and not back down.

One time, we challenged a group of older guys to a

fight. We had maybe ten or fifteen guys on our side against what looked like about twenty of them. My buddy from Vincennes and I led our gang across the bridge. Full of bravado and with our teeth clenched, we began our wobbly trek across the swinging, rope-bridge that separated the two camps. Halfway across, our adversaries stopped. They were laughing and pointing at us! My friend and I turned around, just in time to see the rest of our brave, little gang scampering back to our side. Two against twenty! Not being particularly bright, we looked at each other and boldly continued toward their side.

There was no fight. The big kids smiled, clapped us on our backs and said to us, "you guys have guts! Come on over."

When I was twelve, I got to go to The National Boy-Scout Jamboree, in Colorado Springs, Colorado. That was a great time! We prepared for the trip for what seemed like months. There were detailed instructions on what to take along, what not to take and how to pack everything into a single duffle bag for our journey and stay, at the edge of the Rocky Mountains.

I think there were five or six of us from our area of

Central Illinois going. We stored all our gear in the barn of a farmer whose son was one of our group. He took everything to the train station in his truck and the rest of us caravanned in cars. My first ever train ride!

The train station in Danville, Illinois was our point of departure. Our train was typical of the times. The old fashioned, massive looking, powerful machine with a flared smokestack on top was belching black smoke. We boarded old passenger cars with padded wooden seats. The hugs and tearful goodbyes were reminiscent of a time fifteen years previously when other guys, wearing uniforms, left loved ones on the platform and chugged off on a different kind of adventure.

The train jerked into motion, with steel wheels screeching and cars filled with wide-eyed, excited, young boys. I sat next to a guy from a little farm town, Gilman, Illinois, about fifteen miles from my hometown. Denny Eshleman and I quickly became friends. Football and baseball were his favorite sports, too, so we had a lot to talk about. It didn't take long for us to decide that we would share a tent when we got to Colorado. We gently rocked from side to side and listened to the rhythmic click-clack of the wheels under us, as we looked at the passing corn and soybean fields.

Our train slowed occasionally for a small town and we checked out the backs of stores and warehouses to see cars waiting at crossings. It was a completely different perspective for me and I fogged up our window taking it all in.

Denny and I talked and laughed, or dozed from time to time. We enjoyed the sack lunches which had been prepared for us.

The ride to Kansas City took the entire first day. The city's Union Station was huge, breathtaking; shades of pink marble on the floors and staircases, tall marble pillars reaching toward an arched roof. Every sound echoed through the vast concourse. We ate our meal in the depot cafeteria.

Everything had been coordinated and carefully arranged ahead of time. We had a chance to buy postcards and maybe a magazine before we boarded our train for the last leg of the journey. The scouts bounced along with barely contained excitement but we managed to follow all the instructions despite the driving desire to wander off and explore this new world.

Back aboard, we began to regain some control. Breathing was a little less ragged, heart rates slowed to near normal, and we settled in.

We had 500 miles between us and the Rocky Mountains. From our window, our view of the state of Kansas seemed to never change, hour after hour. Yellow wheat shimmered and swayed, in gentle breezes, for as far as we could see. The tabletop vista was only occasionally broken by a distant grain elevator or a small town.

We slept in our seats through most of Western Kansas and Eastern Colorado. In the morning, a curve in the route gave us a view of hazy, distant mountains in the west. They seemed to magically emerge out of the flat plain. There was no gradual transition from flat to rolling hills and gentle rises. No. A shining wall of purple, then orange, then yellow mountains reflected the morning sun and held us in its magical embrace. Closer and closer they seemed to come. Soon we could see / observe the never-ending north-south wall of majestic peaks. It was a multicolored, jagged wall of rock and snow extending from horizon to horizon. We had arrived!

Our train pulled into Denver. I think it might have been mid-morning when we stretched and lined up, in the aisle, to get off our crowded little train car. Then we stood next to the baggage car and watched porters pass the green duffle bags to our scout leaders, on the platform. Names were called and bags lifted onto shoulders.

We assembled, in a nice little picnic area outside the station and we ate another round of our sack lunches. Soon, buses pulled to the curb and we piled aboard for the journey south to Colorado Springs.

It was a beautiful day, cool and dry. The ride along the edge of the mountains was breathtaking. We gazed at red-sandstone boulders, pine and aspen trees, and at the fast-running streams, splashing and whirling among the smooth rocks, through steep gullies. These natural wonders flashed past our windows. We strained to get a glimpse of some wildlife. Maybe a mountain goat, a bear, or an elk. No such luck that day.

Our destination was a large area adjacent to the United States Air-Force Academy. Before long, the dazzling silver spire of the Academy chapel came into view. The sun reflected off its façade like dancing diamonds. At last, the bus came to a stop. We received some loud and quick instructions, as we shuffled toward the door, "stay together! Keep an eye on your gear and wait for instructions." What we saw, when we dropped our feet onto the reddish, sandy surface can be best described as mass confusion.

The Jamboree was to be home for 56,000 Boy-Scouts for the next two weeks. There were tent cities everywhere. Gravel roads and road signs, with names and numbers, assembly areas, eating and recreation areas. We were all issued maps, a list of rules and regulations, and other interesting tidbits, like exactly how to write the return address on the envelopes when we sent letters home.

We were escorted to our little section and assigned tents. Denny and I shared one. We unpacked our gear and tried to rest. Rest? No way we were going to waste even a minute staying in a stuffy, canvas tent. We were too excited, too ready for adventure. So, we strolled around our tent city getting our bearings, finding out where things were located. The Post Office, bathrooms and showers, the mess tent.

It was easy to know which direction we were heading. The mountains were always to the west. We learned we had been granted access to the Air-Force obstacle course. A day at the obstacle course was scheduled for every group of scouts and by the time our group received its official invitation, Denny and I had run the course dozens of times.

It was a real challenge and definitely intimidating the first couple of times through. Wooden fences to vault over, tubes to crawl through, a high wall to scale, using ropes, irregular beams to balance on and run across, and other cool stuff I cannot remember. What I do remember was that I loved it. The challenge, the competition, the compelling desire to do it better and faster the next time, and of course, the laughing and razzing at one another when we missed a step, lost our grip, or in some fashion, looked goofy. There was a member of the Air-Force assigned to monitor the course, to provide instructions on how to properly navigate a particular obstacle and to ensure the safety of everyone there. Nearly every morning, he would smile at us and say, "you boys back again?"

One day, we met a couple of Scouts, from Texas,

who, like us, couldn't seem to get enough of running the course. Naturally, we competed to see who was the fastest and the races were always close. At the end of the run, we were all in a tight circle, head to head, hands on our knees, breathing hard and sweating like stuck-pigs. All smiles, patting each other on the back and shaking hands. "Hey, y'all wanna go rattlesnake huntin' with us," one of the Texans drawled.

Our response was automatic and in perfect unison, "sure!"

At an orientation meeting early on, we were warned to be careful of rattlesnakes, to watch where we walked and to back away if we saw one. So, when a couple of guys from Texas suggested we go out trying to find them, instead of trying to stay away from them, what do you think a couple of dumb flatlanders from Illinois did? Right! We went rattlesnake hunting. I was not a big fan of snakes and they still scare the hell out of me but showing weakness was not an option. The Texas guys were a little older than us. Their weapons were long sticks with a fork on one end and hunting knives. They knew just where to go, based on the time of day and the angle of the sun in the sky. They told us the best time to catch them was when they were warming themselves on a flat rock in the sunshine. Denny and I watched as the two Texas guys, I don't remember their names, creeped up on a snake sunning himself. One pinned the snake's head with the forked stick. The other Texan calmly reached down and grabbed the snake just behind its head. The diamond-patterned, three-foot-long monster writhed and twisted its long, scaly body, violently.

We stepped back reflexively and watched, in awe and horror, while our Texas buddy wrenched the snakes head, killing it. He proudly held it up and said, "he will make a nice hat-band. Have you ever tried fried rattlesnake? It's pretty darn good." This was not a source of protein I had previously eaten and it didn't sound very appealing at that time but years later I discovered that it is really quite tasty.

My last fond memories of the Boy-Scout Jamboree, were the tour of the Air-Force Academy and getting to see a President of the United States, in person. The tour was kind of boring until we went to the magnificent chapel. Tall, majestic, gleaming silver, a spire rising far into the sky. Inside were beautiful, stained-glass windows, reflecting brilliant sunlight, in a kaleidoscope of dancing colors across the polished floor. A huge organ sat in a corner near the altar with golden pipes, of various lengths, standing at attention, above the three-tiered keyboard.

On one of the last days of the jamboree, President Eisenhower came to visit. I had never been in the presence of a President (never pass up an opportunity to make use of alliteration, I always say). All 56,000 of us were packed along a roadway, as he came riding toward us. He sat atop the back seat of a sleek and shiny, black convertible, waving and smiling, as the car drove by. He wore a light-tan suit and had a brimmed hat perched jauntily on his head. What an experience for a twelve-year-old boy!

During those two weeks in Colorado, I packed a lot of fun, made some great friends and built a ton of wonderful memories.

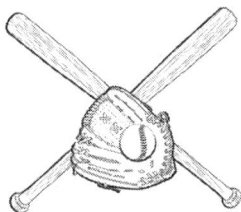

Mercurochrome, Doctors, Cures, and Play

Like all kids, I got banged up from time to time. Black eyes, a bloody nose, skinned knees, cut fingers, all the usual stuff. There were band-aids and Mercurochrome handy at all times. My mom probably bought that nasty, reddish-orange stuff by the gallon. If somebody got dinged during one of our baseball games, we fell back on the age-old and reliable, baseball-cure for everything. "Just rub some dirt on it!"

Occasionally, a doctor's care was required. I had my tonsils taken out when I was six. I had to breathe in this sweet-smelling stuff and the next thing I knew I was in a hospital bed. My mouth was dry, my throat hurt, and a nurse kept bringing me ice-cream.

I remember, one time, I was staying with my grammy Samaras. My parents were playing Bridge or something. Grammy's yard was an explorer's paradise. She had a brick incinerator where she burned her garbage. The garage was dark and musty and full of stuff I had never seen. A sharp, curved tool for cutting weeds, an old double-bladed axe, heavy hammers, and lots of really neat stuff. It was kind of scary in there but I had to check it out. Once, I cut myself on a nail and grammy took me to see her doctor. I remember that he was a nice man, even though he had to give me a shot. His name was Dr. Kosiak. He spoke with a funny accent and I had a hard time understanding what he was saying. He also had some faded numbers tattooed on one of his arms. It wasn't until years later that I understood what those numbers meant.

Our own family doctor was Dr. Hammond. He and my dad knew each other from the war. His office was only a block away from our house and it was right next to his own house, which looked like a castle.

When I was seven, I had a sore throat. Dr. Hammond came to the house with his little black bag. He stuck a stick in my mouth and told me to say, "ahhhh." I heard him tell my mother, "it's strep." He gave us some medicine which I had to take for several days and he'd told mommy that strep could lead to Scarlet Fever, then Rheumatic Fever, and possibly Rheumatic Heart Disease. He recommended that my physical activity be limited for one year.

Like any mother would be, mine was frantic with worry and Dr. Hammond's recommendation became an unbreakable rule carved in stone. No baseball, no bike riding, no swimming-pool, no nothing that I wanted to do. I had to be in the house almost all the time. What could I do? I filled coloring books, I built model airplanes and ships. Dad made it a point to stop by Murphy's many times to bring me something new. I built a model Spitfire, a Navy Grumman Hellcat, a model of the USS Missouri, and a PT Boat. Also, I read some good books, mostly about baseball. My parents decided it would be a good time for me to start taking piano lessons. I hated it but I managed to suffer through the ordeal.

Dr. Hammond said I was okay but then I came down with the measles and had to stay in a dark room. I spent most of the time in mom and dad's bedroom, lying on their big, soft bed, with all the window shades pulled down.

Another time, one of the kids at school got the chicken-pox. All the mothers around wanted to get their own kids exposed; so that they could cross that childhood disease off the list of things they had to worry about. I caught it. Chicken-pox is way worse than the measles. Chicken-pox itch! I was covered with red spots, and my mom dabbed each one with a stinky, pink lotion that was supposed to help. I was miserable, I looked ridiculous and I itched! A lot! Naturally, I had to scratch and I did, whenever I could get away with it. I just had to do it no matter how hard mom tried to stop me. Finally, she put white cotton gloves on my hands to try to make me stop. Lucky for me, I never got the mumps.

The usual childhood diseases out of the way didn't mean I was finished getting banged up or from seeing Dr. Hammond coming through our front door. One time, on a cold, rainy day, Paul and I were shooting baskets in the driveway. It was so cold and damp that the ball got stuck in the net and wouldn't drop. We were a long way from being big enough to jump up and swat the ball loose. Paul grabbed a garden hoe from the garage and swung it high over his head. He got the ball down and he also got me right above my left eye. Blood flowed. Paul screamed. I didn't. I tried to chase him to get a little revenge but mom caught me and I was off to see my favorite doctor... again. I still have the scar and it's a beauty.

There was another favorite thing in my life when I was a boy. My bike! Many years have passed but I can still close my eyes and see it leaning on its kickstand, as though it is still waiting for me. The red Schwinn, a beautiful, mechanical, magic carpet, was always ready to take me on an adventure. When it was new, it was shiny, with red fenders and it had perfect, smooth grips, on the bright, chrome handlebars. The wire basket on the front carried the important items I needed for my day. Sometimes it held a football, maybe a couple of baseballs and all too often, my piano-lesson books. School books and completed homework assignments were a necessary burden during the school year.

It wasn't long before the fenders and the basket were gone, dented or broken after one of the many crashes or wipeouts the bike and I weathered from time to time. Then, it was always about speed. I had places to go and I needed to get there fast. "Wanna race me?" was always a challenge I accepted from one of my buddies.

That extra piece of toast, with apple butter for breakfast, meant I had to "turn and burn," to make it to school on time, or get to my piano lesson. I had to hustle to avoid the wrath of old Mrs. Blankenship, my piano teacher. She scared me. Always had. She taught my dad to play when he was a young boy like me; so, she was old. I thought she was mean, too. She never trusted I had practiced enough. Sitting in a chair next to the piano, in her old, smelly house, she constantly complained about everything I did. "Keep your fingers curved! Get your wrists up! You're in the key of G. That's an F-Sharp. You have a recital in two weeks and you are nowhere near ready." I hated this! Time and again, I sneaked a peek at the old clock on her mantle. Fifteen more minutes!? My groan was silent but my face gave it away. She cast me that 'look'. The look that says, "why can't you get this? You are wasting my time." After an exasperated sigh, she would spit, "from the beginning." Those were the worst words in the world back then.

Finally, it was over. Mentally impatient, I watched

her taking my book and marking it up with her blue pencil. Marks that indicated all the mistakes I made, meaning how completely hopeless I was. I knew, my dad would see those blue scratches and shake his head in resignation.

I couldn't get out of that place of torture fast enough. My beautiful bike just outside old Mrs. Blankenship's front door beckoned; "hop on, let's ride!" I raced up 4th to Lincoln Street, my street and carved a hard right onto the familiar red bricks. Always bumpy, shiny and slick after a rain, that was my territory. I've got a dime in my pocket; so, I would skid to a stop in front of Passon's, the little neighborhood grocery store. It was on my way home and they sold baseball cards. Ten cents will buy me two packs. Five cards and one really brittle and nasty piece of bubblegum. Chewing it, I settled at the picnic table in front of the store and ripped into the packs. Any Cub player was an automatic "keeper". Most of the others would be attached, by a clothes-pin, to the spokes, in the wheels of my bike.

Probably worth thousands of dollars in today's market, those cards were ripped to shreds, as they turned my bike into a roaring motorcycle, with the flapping sound they made. I bounced past Bruce Burton's house on the way home. To my luck, sometimes, he was outside messing around. "Hey Burdy! Get your glove. I'll be back in a minute!"

Home and another skidding stop by the front door. Inside, I dropped my piano books on the bench, then pounded up the stairs to get my ball glove. "Davey, is that you? How was your lesson?", mom's voice would come from the kitchen.

"Fine, I'm going out to play catch with Burdy. Okay?"

"Go ahead. Make sure you are home by the time the streetlights come on."

Boom! I was gone.

Burdy, my pal. We've known each other since first-grade, been walking or riding our bikes to school for the past four years. We did lots of stuff together like, play marbles, throw snowballs, get in trouble in school, play "army, cowboys and indians", play football, ride out to Steely's creek to explore and to throw rocks at the trains rumbling across the trestle bridge, and play baseball. Often, just the two of us playing catch in his front yard.

Playing catch! This was when time would stand still. Throwing that beautiful white ball, feeling the red seams on my fingertips, stepping and moving my left arm in the perfect arc which sends the ball on a path of dreams and imagination.

Sometimes, I imagined myself as Sandy Koufax, sometimes Warren Spahn, or maybe Johnny Podres. I have seen them all play against the Cubs in Wrigley Field. They were lefties like me and I tried to copy everything I saw them do on the field. I knew. I just knew, that someday, it would be me out on that field doing what I had seen them doing.

Then, I felt the ball slap into my leather glove when Burdy threw it back. My glove was shiny, dark-brown leather, with fat fingers. It looked like a pancake. My dad had bought it at Marshall Fields. It was perfect. I loved the way it smelled and how it fitted my hand. The pocket was worn and starting to get thin but I didn't care. Playing catch was automatic. We did it almost without thinking.

We talk while we play. Plans for the next day, some new toy one of us got or wanted, "how did you do on the spelling test? I saw you walking Sarah home yesterday."

Important guy stuff like that. And all the while, throwing each other ground balls and pop ups.

I morphed into Ernie Banks. Burdy became Nellie Fox. It was always the Cubs against the White Sox, in the World Series, for us. Before long, the game could turn into "Burnout". We kept throwing to each other as hard as we could. Burnout was My Game!

Remember, I had been throwing everything I could get my hands on, since I was four. Nobody could beat me in a game of Burnout. On that day, it was no exception. Burdy took off his glove and shook his beet-red hand. Game was over when the streetlights sputtered to life. "See ya!"

"See ya!"

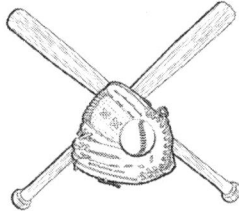

Christmas

Holidays! The big one was Christmas. The anticipation started early, when December's Christmas catalogs started showing up in the mail. Sears, Montgomery Ward, and Marshall Field's catalogs were poured over with a zeal that would have awed my teachers at school. I practically memorized the toy and sporting goods sections of each one. My mom and dad asked for a "wish list". I complied, with enthusiasm. There was Christmas music on the record player and later on the radio. I sat in the classroom and counted down the days until Christmas vacation.

There was the traditional and tortuous annual Christmas program at school. My classmates and I lisped through a tiresome rendition of; "We Wish You a Merry Christmas", to close the program.

Christmas cookies! Oh yeah, Christmas cookies! My mom and grandmommy Brown baked and baked. Sugar cookies of all shapes and sizes, santas, bells, balls, stockings, Christmas trees, and gingerbread men. Then came the icing. Green, white, red, and all kinds of colorful sprinkles. Round, metal Christmas cans were filled with them. Layer upon layer, each separated by a sheet of waxed paper. They were great cookies, no doubt about it but the absolute best Christmas cookies in the entire universe were my grammy Samaras' Greek Christmas cookies.

"Kourabiethes" were crescent shaped, creamy, light, slightly scented with anise and ouzo, creations slowly baked, then richly smothered with powdered sugar. Eating them over the kitchen sink was the best way but not necessarily considered socially acceptable. Most of the time, we wallowed in clouds of powdered sugar, liberally distributing it all over the house and all over our clothes. Wearing dark clothing was contraindicated when coming to grammy's house at Christmas.

The taste of her cookies is impossible to accurately describe. Try to imagine putting something into your mouth that instantly satisfies, excites, and exquisitely tortures all of your senses. If you can picture that and good luck doing that, you will still fall short of the actual experience of eating one of these beauties. One? Did I say, "one!" No one has ever eaten just one. Grammy made them by the hundreds and still they ran out long before we were satiated.

Soon, it would come the time for a family outing to the Christmas-tree market set up in a downtown parking lot. Picking out the perfect tree was an intricate process. Short needles, long needles, was it tall enough, was it straight enough? How long ago was it cut? Lots of questions for the farmer selling his trees. The final decision always rested with my mother, since the house was her domain and everything in it had to be just the way she wanted it. The bedroom, occupied by my brother and I, was a glaring exception but that is another story.

After tying the tree to the roof of the car, we would head for home. While the decision was being made where to put it and which pieces of furniture needed to be moved, we set it in a bucket of water on the back porch. We usually put the tree up shortly after Thanksgiving. Dad carried down the beautiful, old, thin, glass ornaments, previously stored in the attic. Strings of hopelessly tangled lights, with multicolored bulbs, most of which had burned out, had to be untangled and inspected.

Everyone had a job to do. Mine consisted mostly of; "put that down. Be careful where you walk and we're not ready for those yet." What my brother and I did get to do was put the tinsel on the branches, those ridiculously thin strips of some kind of silver paper, maybe aluminum foil. They were about a foot long and were supposed to simulate icicles hanging from the branches. We never saw that effect because before long, we were flinging handfuls of the stuff, at the tree, in the general direction of any bare branch. Done! Beautiful! Another step completed on the long journey to the "Big Day".

Over the next several days, more and more wrapped packages appeared under the tree. Those with our names on them had to be hefted and closely examined. We shook and carefully inspected each present for the slightest clue as to what might be inside. My dad took us shopping to pick out things for mom, and mom performed the reciprocal of that exercise.

Tuffin, our collie shepherd and constant companion, reclined under the tree, as its guardian. Her tail in constant motion, she shared in our growing excitement.

A visit, to meet Santa Claus, was next on the agenda. He sat in a big chair in front of a giant gingerbread house on Main Street. We waited in line to assure him that we had been good boys all year long, then we recited the litany of things we wanted him to bring us. We believed in him completely. I refused to believe some of my friends when they sagely advised me that he wasn't real. I still refuse to believe it. He can be as real as I want him to be and to this day, there are presents under the tree for Mary Lee and me from Santa.

Christmas Eve, the hours dragged on. When will it be time to go to bed, I thought? Is 7:30 too early? We sat up with our parents, drinking hot chocolate out of cute little Santa mugs, eating Christmas cookies, and listening to Christmas music. Paul and I put out milk and cookies for Santa. Finally, we got permission to go to bed, with the gentle warning that, "the faster you go to sleep, the sooner

Santa will be here." Sleep? Who can sleep? We listened for the sound of sleigh-bells and whispered about what we might find under the tree.

With the yellow rays of the emerging sun, the frost on the window began to faintly sparkle. It seemed our dad heard us getting out of bed, so mom came upstairs and said that we had to wait.

"Wait?!"

"Yes, wait until your dad sets up his floodlights and the movie camera. When he's ready, you can go down."

Dad took pictures of everything and the Christmas movies were a major production. We tumbled down the stairs into blinding light. Until our eyes adjusted, there were only our parents' voices, "looks like somebody was here last night."

"Where did all of this stuff come from?"

"Okay, boys, come on down."

The stuff of dreams! Some years there was a sled or a tricycle. Later there would be a new bike, a Lone Ranger gun and holster set, a chemistry set, or Lincoln logs. Santa came through big time! He always did.

By midmorning, the lights had been turned off, the

room was waist deep in empty boxes and wrapping paper. Mom and dad enjoyed their coffee while we tried to figure out what to play with next. After some time, dad commanded, "okay boys, time to clean up this mess. Get everything picked up. You can pile your presents under the tree. Stuff all the garbage into one or two boxes and set them on the back porch." Dad's manner of speaking was liberally sprinkled with Navy terminology and colorful expressions. When we "turned to", we got to work and when we were "squared away", everything was in its proper place. Like a couple of sailors, under the watchful eye of the Captain, we hustled around and had everything cleaned up in no time. We "turned to" until everything was "squared away".

Time to get ready to go over to grandpa Samaras' house for Christmas dinner. We got dressed up and were allowed to take one toy each with us.

Grandpa's house looked like a mansion to me. Everything was big. Big easy chairs, big couches, a big grand-piano, a big dining-room table, and big sideboards loaded down with food. Not just any food but, Greek food! Walking through their front door would make even the pickiest eater salivate. Aromas of lemon juice, olive-oil, garlic, chicken, and lamb permeated the senses. Grammy's meals were legendary. We had appetizers of feta cheese, Kalamata olives and anchovies, while the finishing touches to the feast were being tended to in the kitchen.

Grammy and grandpa had been cooking since the night before and all morning. The polished, to a bright shine, silver and the fine-china was laid out on a starched, snow-white, lace tablecloth. There were bottles of Retsina and Roditis for the adults, while we had Welch's grape juice poured into our crystal, wine goblets. Spanakopita, my favorite, red potatoes, spaghetti, and green beans, Greek style (Fasolakia Gianzi) were the side dishes to go with the lamb, slowly cooked in lemon juice, olive oil, and garlic and baked chicken, which had been prepared in much the same way.

Nothing and I mean nothing, compares with those Christmas dinners. Grandpa recited a brief blessing in his native tongue and we began. Everyone clinked glasses with the traditional Greek Christmas greeting, Kala Hristouyienia! We, children, used our best table manners and we all ate slowly, savoring every bite. Around the table, eyes were glazed over in ecstasy. Grammy received a well-deserved compliment after nearly every mouthful. We always followed up those compliments with requests for seconds.

No one ever leaves a Greek household hungry. Ever! Afterwards, the kids were excused from the table, while the grownups took care of the cleanup. The crystal and the china were too delicate for our fumbling fingers. That's why we had been allowed to bring one of our new toys. Later, there was baklava and coffee for the adults and ice-cream, with grandpa's chocolate syrup and a hidden stash of Greek Christmas cookies, for us.

Afterwards, my dad would take his place at the piano and entertain us. Requests were shouted, acknowledged, and played entirely from memory. I loved standing next to him, watching his nimble fingers flying over the keys. Finally, time would come to go home. Hugs and kisses all around, everyone happy, tired, and stuffed.

This is how I remember my boyhood Christmases.

DAVID SAMARAS

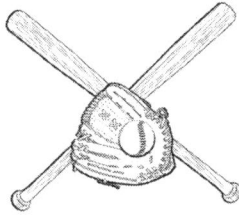

Other Holidays

Our birthdays were less than a month after Christmas. Paul's was on January 17 and mine on the 19th. We always celebrated them together. After the orgy of toys, games, and sports equipment we amassed at Christmas, birthday gifts were far more practical and by that, I mean, yawn-inducing. Underwear and socks, shirts and pants, were the usual birthday fare. The grandparents always came through with the good stuff, like a couple of items that Santa may have overlooked. Always a cake, always chocolate, with chocolate icing, a rousing, sometimes harmonious rendition of "Happy Birthday", make a wish, and blow out the candles.

Mother's Day and Father's Day were celebrated

with the off-holiday parent taking us shopping for the guest of honor and since both were late Spring and early Summer holidays and both were held on a Sunday, that meant a trip to Wrigley Field to see a double-header, if the Cubs were in town. That meant getting up early and driving nearly two hours to Chicago to be there for batting practice.

The first game started at twelve-thirty and the second game usually ended around six or six-thirty. It never occurred to us that mom might not enjoy this outing quite as much as the men in the family; so, on Mother's Day, late in the afternoon, after the games, we took her to the fancy new shopping center on Michigan Avenue – Water Tower Place. Some shopping for mom and dinner at her favorite French restaurant, The Ile de France.

On Father's Day, a month later, we did much the same, except for the choice of a restaurant. We headed down Halstead Street to Greek Town. Dianna's Restaurant and Grocery was my dad's favorite and mine too. Dianna's was something special. The owner, Peter Kogenes, was a real character. Tall, he always wore a white cowboy hat and he had a chrome-plated pistol stuffed into the strings of his sauce-stained apron. He greeted all visitors the same way. A big hug and a loud, heavily accented, "welcome home!" The food there was wonderful. My favorite, was his lamb and spaghetti. The meat was so tender and juicy, it actually fell off the bone. Wine for our parents, cokes for us. It became a tradition that at the end of the meal, he would bring over a bottle of Metaxa; glasses for everyone and he toasted our health.

Grandpa and Peter claimed to be distant cousins but, then, all Greeks seem to be cousins. Several times a year, my dad, grandpa, and the two of us made a special trip to Dianna's so that grandpa could stock up on olives, cheese, bread, olive-oil, wine, and a bunch of things from the grocery, way too hard to pronounce or to remember. After our usual and always memorable lunch, we packed the station wagon and headed home. We did this year after year and we always had a blast.

One time we saw Anthony Quinn enjoying a meal, and another time we saw Milt Pappas, a pitcher for my beloved Cubs. Celebrities always posed with Peter for a picture and those pictures filled every available wall space throughout the restaurant.

I absolutely loved spending time with my grandpa. He always had a smile on his face. His dark, almost black eyes sparkled with humor and his genuine love of life. No one I have ever known worked harder and had more fun doing it. At about the same age as I was doing all the fun things, as a kid, he was on a ship, by himself, sailing to America. It's hard to imagine a nine-year-old boy moving to a strange land where people spoke a language he didn't understand.

His generosity had no bounds. On Easter, he and my grammy had an open house. They cooked and prepared for days while still fasting themselves. After church and all day and evening, their house was open to anyone who wanted to stop by for a meal. People came and went all day. Some stopped in, just for coffee and a desert and some came over and enjoyed a complete meal. Grandpa made it a point to sit down and eat with everyone who came over. That level of commitment did require some sacrifices. He would make periodic trips to the bathroom and force himself to throw up, so he could offer the full measure of Greek hospitality to the next guest.

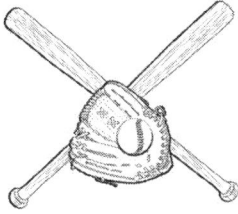

My Mother's Side of the Family - Granddaddy Brown and Grandmommy Brown

I loved my maternal grandparents as much as I loved grandpa and grammy Samaras. Grandmommy and granddaddy Brown moved to Hoopeston from the tiny town of Virden, Illinois, about 180 miles away. My granddaddy Brown opened a Texaco Service station at the intersection of Route One and Route Nine, at the edge of town and grandmommy Brown managed a motel right next to the gas station. I loved spending the night, or sometimes the whole weekend with them. I got to help out at the station. I had one of those reddish, pink rags in my back pocket, just like granddaddy had. I helped him, "fill 'er up", check the oil, and wipe the windshield. There was a black cord running along the ground between the building and the gas pumps. Every time a car drove over it, the bell in the office or the garage would sound, Ding-Ding, Ding-Ding. We would hustle outside and ask, "fill 'er up, Sir?"

Inside the office there was a desk with a black telephone and a usually full ashtray. On the wall, a calendar, with a pretty girl holding some tools, a rack filled with road maps, and a Coke machine. Everything was kind of greasy and carried the smell of oil and gasoline. It was perfect! Besides, there was always country music playing on the radio from KMOX in St. Louis. I can still hear, "...I was dancin' with my darlin' to the Tennessee waltz..."

The big double-doors in the garage went up and down when you pressed a button. Along the back-wall, tools and hoses, tires on racks almost to the ceiling, were stacked. Just inside one of the big doors was a set of silver platforms. A car could drive up on them and stop. Granddaddy pulled a lever and the car went straight up in the air; so, he could see and work on all the stuff underneath. That was a lot of fun to watch. He would twist things with a wrench, pound on things with a rubber hammer, pull out old, brown, rusty things and replace them with new, bright and shiny things. He always whistled while he worked and he taught me how to whistle, too.

At first all I could do was blow spit but finally, one day, I made a sound! I kept at it and before long, I could fashion a tune. So, it was granddaddy and I working and whistling together in the garage. I would hand him things. "No, not that one. The one with the red handle, over there." He got the wrong stuff from me most of the time but he didn't seem to mind.

Sometimes, he would say bad words. I would laugh and he would say, "we won't tell grandmommy about that. Okay?" We didn't. We were working-men doing working-men stuff. When we took breaks, we drank cokes from the red coke machine. A nickel and a penny bought an ice-cold coke, in a heavy glass bottle. We would take a swig, then wipe our mouths with our sleeves, and sigh, "aaahhh!" You know, guy stuff.

At the end of the day, it was time to clean up and go home. Granddaddy would say, "let's go wash up." We dipped our fingers into a big can of yellow, greasy stuff and rubbed it all over our hands and arms. That took care of most of the grease and oil. Next, we stood at the iron sink and turned on the warm water. There was a big, gray bar of Lava Soap on the edge. It felt gritty rubbing it between my hands but it produced a lot of nice smelling lather. We got ourselves cleaned up and closed the station for the night.

We walked across the lot to grandmommy's house, whistling all the way. Even before we opened the front door, we were treated to the heavenly aroma of a pot-roast in the oven, along with carrots, chunks of potato and onions. There was brown gravy keeping warm on the stove and a cherry pie, cooling on the windowsill above the sink.

Grandmommy always smiled. She and granddaddy were survivors of the Great Depression. Most of their lives they struggled with poverty and low-paying jobs. They were forced to make frequent moves but she had the ability to create a comfortable home out of the worst of circumstances. Everything was clean, always inviting, always meticulously cared for. My dear grandmommy had an old, Singer sewing-machine that she operated by pushing on a treadle near the floor. She made clothes for herself and her family, sewed curtains, knitted sweaters and caps, and even warm blankets. Even with a very limited income some of the time, they never thought of themselves as poor.

When I wasn't working at the station, I was exploring. Behind the motel was a big field. Early in the summer, asparagus grew there and migrant workers, with long, narrow, wicker baskets picked it, called it snapping and dumped it into bins, which were transported to the canning factory.

After the season was over, I roamed through the field looking for interesting rocks and arrowheads, or anything else that would catch my eye. There always were few stalks of asparagus left to snap and chew on, while I walked. There were plenty of nice dirt clods to pick up and throw. For a little kid, those were days well spent and ones I still love to remember.

DAVID SAMARAS

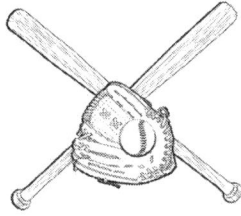

A Change of Address

Just before I started the 7th Grade, my family moved from Hoopeston to Watseka, 25 miles to the north. Watseka was a nice town, about the same size as Hoopeston but it somehow seemed to be a little more affluent. I'm not sure I can explain it. Everything looked neater and cleaner. The houses seemed to be bigger and more elegant and the whole atmosphere was inviting.

We moved during the summer. My dad opened his second restaurant there. It was an exact replica of the Ritz in Hoopeston and it was in a perfect location, right in the middle of the business district. But before it opened, there was a traumatic event.

Dad was working late in the afternoon sawing some

wood. Somehow, his hand slipped, and the whirring table-saw took off his left thumb and little finger. The owner of the butcher shop next door heard the cries for help and rushed over. Mr. Williams wrapped the bleeding hand in towels, searched for and found the little finger and put it in a bag of ice. He then rushed my dad to the local hospital.

The thumb was gone, severed at the first joint leaving only a stub. The surgeon was able to reattach the little finger. It would be forever immobile but my dad asked him to set it in a curved position so that he could still play the piano.

I know dad was devastated but he never let it show. Quiet strength and leadership were on display, for me to absorb and hopefully put to use one day. The restaurant opened on time, the bandages were removed and the piano continued to fill our home with beautiful music. Dad accepted the setback and found a way to overcome what might have been a significant disability.

I don't remember having any difficulty leaving my old friends and making new ones. None of us ever considered the possibility that the last time we played together would indeed be the last time. In Watseka, I had most of the summer to get acquainted. The park and the city pool were an easy bike ride away. Our neighborhood was filled with kids around my age and there was baseball. Watseka was my home until I finished high-school. It was the beginning of a new decade, the 60s, one that would come to have a special significance for most of us.

As for me, I just plowed through it and tried to have fun. I kicked ass on occasion, got mine kicked from time to time, did lots of stupid shit and made some great friends.

My Middle-School was only two blocks from the downtown area, so, on my lunch hour, I walked to the Ritz and worked behind the soda-fountain counter. There were eight stools and they were usually occupied by local businessmen eating lunch. I poured coffee into heavy china cups, scribbled orders on my guest-check pad, barked those orders to the cook nearby, kept the counter and the fountain area spotless, with a white cheese-cloth rag, and I always suggested a piece of pie for dessert. The pies! They were something special. All homemade, every morning, by a woman named Ethel. She was a serious, old lady, with snow-white hair, a colorful apron, lightly coated with flour and a gift for making the most delicious pies in the world. Coconut cream, banana cream, chocolate cream, apple, cherry, rhubarb, mincemeat. Her crusts were so incredibly flaky and mouth-watering, the meringues towered over the cream pies, always white with a light tan searing on the top.

My job was to serve lunches at the counter and to, "…push the pie…". I pushed but I never had to push very hard. Most of the customers were regulars and a piece of Ethel's pie was something to be savored. I picked up a few dimes and quarters, as tips, for my outstanding service and gobbled down my own lunch and the piece of pie I had hidden away, before heading back to school.

On weekends, I was able to perfect and show off my soda-jerking skills. I remember many sunny, summer days walking from our house up Fourth Street. I could listen to bits and pieces of the Cub's game along the way. It seemed like most of the houses I passed, there was a man sitting on his porch listening to the radio broadcast of the game. Behind the counter, I was ready to go. At the Ritz, I would change into a white shirt, with the sleeves rolled up to my elbows and with a white apron tied around my waist. People came in for ice-cream sodas, parfaits, sundaes, milkshakes and malts, banana-splits, and fountain drinks of a wide variety of flavors.

One of the little tricks I learned was to crack a raw egg into the shakes and malts to make them extra smooth and creamy. My personal favorite and my own invention was, the hot-fudge malt with peppermint ice-cream. Oh yeah!

I always had a lot of fun working at the Ritz for my dad. But I remember one time, late in the afternoon, shortly before I was to be relieved, two school busses pulled up in front of the restaurant and began disgorging kids. It was a Boy-Scout troop, or something, coming back from Chicago on an outing. On the way home, they decided to stop in Watseka for a snack. I must have made fifty milkshakes that afternoon.

Each shake was made the same meticulous way. There were no shortcuts. Two or three scoops of ice-cream dropped into the stainless-steel Hamilton-Beach can, a few ounces of milk, the syrup of the flavor of choice, and my special raw egg. The can would then be slid up under the blades of the blender. The high-pitched whine and the whirling blades soon rendered a perfect milkshake.

Washing and rinsing the can and wiping down the blades were all part of the process. Over and over I repeated that process on that particular day. When I walked home, I think I carried half the contents of the soda fountain splattered across my shirt.

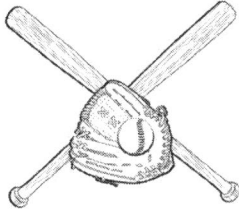

Moving Up to Babe-Ruth League

My 7th and 8th Grade years were dominated by baseball. It was a fall sport for us. Our coach was in his first year, a young guy fresh out of college, where he'd played on the Varsity. We were a good team. No, we were a great team. We lost one game in two years and we pretty much dominated the competition around the county. I will never forget the time Coach called me and my catcher aside after practice and said, "you two are going to play in the Major Leagues someday." It never happened for either of us but what an ego boost for a couple of young boys with dreams!

Summers in Watseka were spent much the same way they had been in my old hometown. We played baseball, whiffle ball, hung out at the swimming pool, played kick-the-can. Of course, for me, baseball took precedence.

We moved to Watseka after my last Little-League season. In my new town I moved up to Babe-Ruth league. It was quite a shock that first season. In Little-League the pitching distance is 46-feet and the bases are 60-feet apart. In Babe-Ruth league, it is a full-sized field. The pitching distance is 60-feet-six-inches and the bases are 90-feet apart. I was a pitching stud in Little-League but in my first season on the full-sized, regulation baseball field, I didn't win a single game. From the mound, home plate looked like it was a mile away. My fastball that mowed them down in Little-League became easy meat for the 14 and 15-year-old guys I faced in Babe-Ruth ball.

I was fortunate to have a good coach that first year. He instilled in me that in order to be successful, I had to learn to deal with setbacks, disappointments, and failure. He also taught me the importance of learning how to make the necessary adjustments in order to stay competitive. He taught me a pickoff move that was probably a balk but I learned it and picked off 13 base-runners that first season.

I learned how to throw a curveball and a change-up, to compensate for my anemic fastball. I still teach the pickoff move to my left-handed high-school pitchers and it still works like a charm.

That first season was good for me because it forced me to deal with disappointment and humiliation on the field. That was a hard lesson for me because I have always been fiercely competitive and was often my own worst enemy. I would get mad at myself for making a mistake and losing focus and concentration. I could accept mistakes and errors from my teammates but I had a hard time forgiving myself for not being good enough.

My 7th grade season in Middle-School gave me a boost. I won every game I pitched and the team went undefeated. My next year of Babe-Ruth, I worked hard not to suck. And I didn't. Over the winter, I had gotten a little bigger and a lot stronger. More important was the fact that the dismal season the year before helped me to become mentally tougher. I made the All-Star team that second season and I set a Babe-Ruth league strikeout record that lasted for ten years. I mowed down seventeen hitters in a seven-inning game.

Naturally, I still remember that game in some detail. Our coach had a strict rule that no one was to go swimming on game day. I had forgotten that we had a game that night and I spent the whole afternoon at the pool. By game time, I was tired and my eyes stung from the chlorine. I knew that I was not, "...bringing my A-Game...", when I warmed up to start the game. I also think that my condition made me concentrate more on what I was trying to do. It also helped that the opposition that night had a lineup loaded with left-handed batters. I eat lefties for lunch! I threw lots of knee buckling curve balls that night. I struck out one kid, a friend of mine, three times while his mom spent the evening standing behind the screen yelling at the home-plate umpire. It was a beautiful thing!

The whiffle ball games rose to a new level. Many of them took place in our front yard. We stuck a yellow pole in the drain spout, on the corner of the porch, for the right-field foul pole. The leftfield line was the sidewalk going north past "Big Julie's" house. Hitting balls into her yard were home runs. They were also almost impossible to retrieve. She was mean but her screened, front porch paid the price, on Halloween night. Something about some eggs splattered on it. Of course, we knew nothing about that.

Anyway, most of the whiffle ball games were one-on-one affairs. In Watseka, you were either a Cub fan or a White Sox fan, so, when we squared off it was always the Cubs against the Sox. My buddies John or Mike would be everybody in the Sox lineup and I was everybody in the Cub's lineup. We copied batting stances and we filled our cheeks with raisins to look like we were chewing tobacco. Accuracy was as important to us, as squaring up a belt-high fastball and driving it into the next county.

I was starting to learn the subtleties of the game of baseball. I began to realize that the umpire behind the plate is a "King". He could be a good king and give me a called strike on a pitch just off the corner of the plate, or he could be a bad king and miss one that was obviously right down the middle. I learned that arguing with, or in some other way showing disrespect to an umpire, can turn a quiet, sunny day, into a raging thunderstorm, or sometimes turn a pleasant nod of the head into a calm assassination.

My catcher for one season in Babe-Ruth league was a guy named Steve. He was an outstanding athlete and a great guy to have for a teammate. Steve also had a hot temper and when it boiled to the surface, everyone knew it. We were good friends and seeing him get tossed from a game was always one of the setbacks I had to deal with but this one time, I witnessed one of the coolest things I have ever seen an umpire do.

Steve struck out and really looked bad doing it. He threw his bat straight up into the air and I mean he threw it high enough that it sailed past the light tower. The umpire casually took off his mask and looked up. Then, he looked back at Steve and said, "son, if that bat comes down, you're gone." It did and Steve headed for the locker room. I learned that umpires always know two things about any argument on the field. They know who is going to win it and they know exactly how long it will last.

I made it a point to never piss off the "King". I tried to be as gracious as I could be, no matter what I thought of the job he was doing. I wanted my catcher to act the same way. We always sat together in the dugout between innings and sometimes I would remind him that we needed a friend back there, not an enemy. I might say something like, "hey, you two are going to spend about three hours, six inches away from each other. You are both going to be hot and sweaty. Talk to him, chat him up a little. Don't ever question his calls and make sure your body language is always positive. Ask him about his wife or girlfriend and stay cool. He might call a pitch in our favor sometime when we really need it."

Later, when I began coaching, I told my catchers pretty much the same thing. I also insisted that at the beginning of the game they would go to the umpire and introduce themselves, to shake his hand and tell him that they will do their best to keep him from getting dinged by a bad pitch. Maybe that works, maybe not but I have had umpires come to me after games and apologize for missing a call.

The first time that happened to me was when I was still playing. I was in my late twenties by that time and playing on a semi-pro team in Kansas. I was the oldest player on a team of college guys from all over the country. It was a great team! We had five All-Americans on the team and we were hard to beat. I was pitching maybe the best game of my life that day.

We were ahead one to nothing in the ninth inning and I had only given up one hit. Their lead-off hitter got on base with a bunt single that I was not quick enough to chase down and make a play on. A walk and an error loaded the bases. With two outs, I admit it. I was gassed, completely spent. I did not want to throw a fastball anywhere near the strike zone. A right-handed batter stepped to the plate. I threw my curve ball at his back foot. Strike one. He fouled off my two-seam fastball low and away. I tried to go low and away again but missed. Ball one. I threw my changeup and it definitely caught the inside corner but the umpire's right arm did not come up. The count was two and two. I was thinking, 'what next?' I had to throw the ball over the plate and my fastball had left me back in the seventh inning or so. I threw the change again. Same pitch, same location. The hitter thought it was low but the umpire rang him up. Strike three! Game over!

There were handshakes all around, then the umpire walked up to me and offered his hand. "That first change-up you threw was a strike but for some reason I just couldn't make the call. It was a strike and I missed it. You pitched a hell of a game tonight."

Why are these old baseball memories so special to me? Let me try to explain it this way. It's all about the

"Face in the Mirror". When I began coaching high-school baseball players, I discovered that especially among the younger players there came a time early in the season when they became comfortable with the practice routine and what to expect during a game. I noticed that this new comfort level often manifested itself in the form of goofing off during drills, not giving maximum effort, and repetition of mental mistakes. I would call them over to me and say something like this to them:

"Every baseball career ends. Yours will end someday, too. It might end next week, it might end next year, it might end ten years from now. That day comes for all of us. When it does, there will be a time when you see a face in the mirror and you will have a brutally honest discussion. That discussion will go one of two ways. You might sigh and say, 'I wish I had worked harder.' Or, you might face that mirror and say, 'I gave it all I had all the time. I have no regrets. We won games, we lost games, but we always did it together, my teammates and me. I always tried to be a better player and a better teammate. I worked hard every day and I tried to learn as much as I could. I have wonderful memories about my time in the sun.'

Guys, I want you to listen to this old guy. Cherish every moment of this experience. Work to get better every day. Go full speed all the time. Get sweaty, get dirty, work hard and work together. This is your team. This is your time in the sun. Do not waste it. I want all of you to look at that face in the mirror someday and smile, knowing that you gave this game all you had to give."

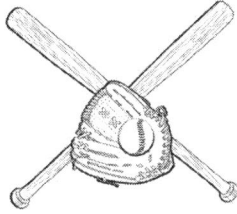

Girls

Girls were becoming more interesting to me. Susie was so cute and she had the best legs in the 7th grade! Her house was just two blocks away and right across the street from the Iroquois County Hospital. Once I had to spend three or four days in the hospital, with some kind of fungus infection on my feet. There was no pain, I just had my feet wrapped in a boric-acid solution and had to stay in bed. My room had a window that faced the garage of Susie's house. We both got flashlights and cards with Morse Code printed on them and signaled back and forth. It was probably the first blush of romance I experienced. Later, we spent a lot of time together trying to figure out what to do next. For some reason we never dated but we always remained friends.

It seemed that when we got to high-school, all the cute freshman girls were scooped up by the upper-class boys and Susie certainly fit the description of cute! She was always a member of the group who played Kick the Can on summer evenings. There was Chip and his little brother, Nancy and her little brother, Diane and Susie plus a couple of kids who lived across the street from us whose names I don't remember. We ran around in the dark hiding from each other. Sometimes boys and girls paired up, only to discover how much more fun it was to do stuff with a pretty girl, than with one of the guys. Times and priorities were changing for us and it was exciting.

Things began to get a little awkward during my junior-high years. Yeah, I was still a stud on the baseball field and school was pretty easy. It was so easy, in fact, that boredom was a major problem and something needed to be done.

Poor old Mrs. Phillips. She was my home-room teacher during eighth grade. She would take the attendance in the morning and be satisfied that every desk was occupied and that every name had a check mark next to it.

She stuffily pivoted her generous girth toward the blackboard to scratch some mindless drivel on the board. When she turned back toward the class, everything would come to an immediate and electrifying halt. She usually stood stock still, the chalk in her hand pointed skyward, her now quivering mouth agape, as she stared at some empty desks now! The rest of my classmates watched, with well-disguised glee, as the dark cloud of confusion swept across her furrowed face.

Crawling out of that first-floor window was ridiculously easy. We were able to do it with the speed and the stealth of a jungle cat. A couple of the guys and I did it many times that year. We would quickly walk around to the front of the school and enter through the front door. We sauntered down the hall, then casually walked into Mrs. Phillips' classroom. "Good morning, Mrs. Phillips!" we sang in unison. The whiskers on her chin danced, with the rhythmic opening and closing of her mouth, as we obediently took our seats. I don't think she ever figured out what we had done and of course we passed our little trick along to the class behind us, when the opportunity presented itself. As a result, our well-earned reputation for outrageous fuckery continued to grow.

Speaking of confusion, our own young lives became more and more confusing on many Friday and Saturday nights. At our age, the girls were more mature, easily more sophisticated than the boys and suddenly a whole lot prettier. Some of the girls in our class organized parties. They were almost always held in someone's finished basement. Stacks of 45rpm records played all the latest rock and roll hits. There were snacks and soft drinks and the hosting parents would make strategically timed, quiet trips down the stairs to make sure all the lights were still turned on and that their worst fears had not been realized. After a while, lights would mysteriously go out and slow-dance songs replaced everything else in the record pile and I was introduced to a whole new world.

Girls were soft. They smelled nice and there were new, emerging and interesting curves. There was a euphoric heat being generated that I liked. A lot! Wow! And I thought baseball was fun!

Parties like this happened almost every weekend. Boys and girls began to pair off and to find dark corners. Lots of fumbling, lots of tentative gestures and clumsy moves. Funny to think about it now but at the time, nothing was more exciting, nothing more frightening, nothing more nerve-wracking. I experienced nervousness the likes of which I had never known. Facing my parents after getting caught doing something especially stupid, taking a pop quiz at school, getting that final-out in a ball game, these were nothing. No problem at all, but this. This, the prospect of kissing a girl, this was akin to staring into the abyss. "What if I do it wrong? What if she doesn't like it? What if she laughs at me?" I didn't realize until sometime later that she was probably going through the same swamp of anxiety and thinking the same things I had been thinking. Lucky for us the girls really were more mature and more sophisticated than us mopes.

Later, amongst the guys, there was the usual bravado, all complete bullshit of course. Eventually, some of us learned to dance fairly well and by that, I mean we didn't fall down and the crushing of female toes became less and less common. We developed a rudimentary concept of rhythm and movement and looked slightly less silly as time went on. The slow songs like, "Put Your Head on My Shoulder" and "I Only Have Eyes for You," were still the crème de la crème and we feasted on them. We thought, or rather I thought, I was ready for high-school. I wasn't. That comes next.

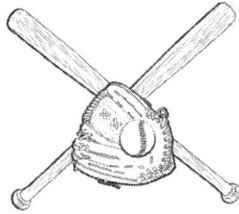

High-School

I began my high-school career in 1962. Watseka Community High-School was the largest school that this small-town boy had ever attended. There were probably 600 students in all and our freshman class numbered around 150.

Watseka was a football town. High-school football there was "King". Every boy who grew up in Watseka dreamed of playing for Coach MacKenzie. He was a true legend. Larger than life, massive thick shoulders, a crew-cut hair style, and piercing eyes that never missed anything.

Of course, I wanted to be a football player. I wanted to be a Watseka Warrior wearing the beautiful maroon and white colors and experiencing glory on the football field on Friday nights. I went out for the football team. Back then, there was no youth football or Pop-Warner football for young kids. My friends and I played our version of the game in back yards around town. Football practice started two or three weeks before the Fall semester began. We practiced twice a day during the blistering heat of August. The morning sessions, 8am to 10am, were manageable; hard but still not too bad. The afternoon practices, from 2pm to 4pm, were just plain brutal! The grassy practice field behind the school quickly turned into a hardened, dusty, heat-reflecting surface, where neither gallons of perspiration, nor some occasional blood could coax anything cool and green to grow.

In the beginning, we were issued high-top football shoes and helmets. We did a lot of running. I mean, we ran everywhere, all the time. Wind sprints, usually in increments of 10 over a forty-yard distance became a test of will and determination as much as a conditioning and evaluation session. The half-mile runs around the track were how we started and ended practice every day. Add to these, a seemingly endless number of diabolical, lung-bursting exercises. Push-ups, sit-ups, up/downs. I can't even remember them all anymore.

I remember that all the tee-shirts, socks, towels, and jock straps we were issued had been dyed a bright pink color. The school provided all the equipment we wore during practices and games, with Coach MacKenzie thinking that the pink dye would prevent players from stealing equipment or taking souvenirs. It didn't work out quite the way he planned. Throughout my high-school days, wearing a pink tee-shirt around town became a sort of "Badge of Honor". "Hey look, there goes a football player!".

After the first week of practice, we were issued our full uniforms. Shoulder pads, hip pads, thigh pads, knee pads, football pants, and jerseys. The "full-pads" practices were an introduction to pain. Pain, the likes of which this skinny little freshman had never known. I learned how to tackle. I learned how to block and I learned how to take massive amounts of physical punishment. I hated it and I loved it! Yeah, I know. That doesn't make any sense. It's hard to understand and even harder to explain. I remember the feeling I had after I had played my last college football game. I said to one of my teammates, "only a crazy man would say this but I know that I will miss those "two-a-days" next August."

He said, "yeah, you're crazy! C'mon let's get out of here and grab a beer."

There was no high-school baseball at WCHS. There were only three Varsity sports; football, basketball and track. Coach MacKenzie was not only the Varsity football coach, he was the track coach and the Athletic Director. To his way of thinking, "if you want to play football for me in the Fall, you had better go out for track in the Spring. There was no room for baseball in that program. That meant that my high-school athletics were limited to football and track. I had no interest in playing basketball.

School starts at the end of August. I was part of a long line of nervous freshmen getting our class schedule. Friends were comparing notes to see if they might be in some classes together. All around, there are upper-classmen checking out the new crop. The junior and senior jocks were preparing to snatch up the cutest of the freshman girls. The upper-class girls, many of them tall, beautiful, and long legged, in their short skirts are waving at us hapless boys, blowing kisses, and in countless other ways, adding to our already high level of angst. High-school was about to become an experience like no other.

While we had only three varsity sports available to us at WCHS, the school offered a good variety of academic and vocational programs. There were also instrumental and vocal music programs. All of my courses were of the "College Preparatory" type. As I recall, only two foreign languages were offered, Spanish and Latin. At that time, my scholarly aspiration was to become a physician. Since I wanted to be a doctor, I decided (that is, my parents decided) to take Latin, along with all the basics, Math, Science, English, History, and Geography. Latin was fairly easy but mind-numbingly boring. We learned to read and write in Latin but there was no speaking portion. Reading about Julius Caesar was a major yawn-inducing experience.

My favorite classes were History and English. It took me a while to catch on to the concept of Algebra but when that, "aha moment" came, I started to enjoy it. During my four years, I took all the mathematics classes the school offered. My science courses included Biology,

Chemistry, and Physics, along with the basic General Science course for freshmen. Physics was my favorite because of all the cool experiments we watched and sometimes got to set up and conduct ourselves.

I loved my History, English and English-Literature classes the most, partly because of my teachers and partly because of the subject matter. There was another distinct advantage to taking these classes. They required lots of research and research meant making trips to the Public Library, after school, in the evenings. I could meet my friends there, maybe actually do some work and check out the girls who were supposed to be doing the same assignments we were supposed to be doing. Later, after some of us received our coveted driver's license, going to the library meant riding around town and engaging in activities which were decidedly non-academic. These forays always took place after a brief, token visit, to the library, just so we could honestly report that we had been there.

I was involved in the music program, as a singer. I was a member of the Boys' Chorus, the Mixed Chorus and the Boys' Quartet. Much of the Fall semester every year was devoted to learning Handel's "Messiah". At the end of the semester, at the annual Christmas program, we performed several of the choruses and arias. Because of my years of taking (albeit hating) piano lessons, I could read music and I guess I had a decent tenor voice. Some of my dad's passion for music must have been passed on to me because singing in those programs was something I thoroughly enjoyed. The fact that the Mixed Chorus seemed to always be filled with gorgeous girls may have been a factor in my elation, at the prospect of rehearsals and performances. Yeah, I'm sure that was a huge factor.

School days during the Fall semester were long. Football players were at the school at 7am. Before the game schedule started, we sat in a classroom and studied the playbook. Each player had to know the assignment of every position, on every play and there were a lot of plays!

Once the season started, we watched films of our previous game and film of our next opponent. Sometimes those film sessions were brutal! Coach would run a play forward and backward, over and over, pointing out mistakes, missed tackles, missed blocks, blown assignments. On the occasions where I was the culprit, I could feel myself melting into the desk-chair upon which I sat. These morning meetings were intense, no-nonsense sessions and heaven help the guy who showed up a minute late for one.

School started at 8:30 and ended at 4:00pm. Football practice began at 4:30 and ended at 6 or 6:30. Monday, Tuesday and Wednesday practices were always the toughest. Lots of contact, lots of hitting, and lots of yelling from the coaching staff. When, a few years later, when I was struggling and becoming discouraged when I was trying to make the football team at Illinois, one of the upper-classmen told me that as long as a coach is yelling at you, you are doing fine. It's when he stops yelling at you that you need to worry. Anyway, those first three days of practice every week were especially hard if we'd lost the game the previous Friday night. Thursday practices were light and easy. No pads. Just walking through the game plan and making sure we were ready for Friday.

I was usually whipped, worn out and dragging, by the time I got home from school. My mom always had a delicious meal ready and the whole family always ate together. After dinner, I did my assigned kitchen duty then got busy on my homework. When I think about it now, it seems like a rough schedule to keep but at the time it was just the normal routine.

The social life for this freshman was even more daunting. In the two years I lived in Watseka before high-school, I had made many good friends. In high-school, some of us shared classes, some were on the football team, some in chorus. For the most part, upper-classmen ignored us but there were a few exceptions. I was the only freshman in the Boys' Quartet. A fact that probably had more to do with adolescent voice changes than musical talent but I became friends with the older guys and we had a lot of fun together. We sometimes performed around town, at various civic clubs, or at the local nursing-home.

Most Friday and Saturday nights, there were dances in the gym. They were called "Sock Hops" because everyone had to remove their shoes, so as not to scuff up the gym floor. There was music, dancing and refreshments, usually compliments of one of the school clubs. Mostly, the freshman boys just stood around and watched as the upper-classmen began snatching up the cutest of our female classmates. We still managed to have fun; joking around, trying to act cool, and generally behaving like the immature idiots we all were. We also realized that once we became upper-classmen, our time would come.

Friday-night football was a huge event in Watseka. The freshman team played their game right after school. The Junior Varsity played a game at around 6pm. Then the Varsity game began at around 8pm.

My first year of high-school football was decidedly unspectacular. I wasn't good enough. I got to play sporadically and there were a couple of games in which I rode the bench the whole time. I was frustrated and disappointed but my dad had a simple solution. "If you want to play, you have to get better." I wanted to play! I cleverly concluded that the guys who were playing ahead of me, were always bigger and faster than I was. I had little control over getting bigger, so, I decided that I needed to become a faster runner.

I found a paperback book published by "Sports Illustrated" magazine on, "How to Become a Better Sprinter". I studied it diligently. I practiced the movements, tried to attain the proper body lean, the right way to coordinate arm swings with leg movement, high knees, springing from the balls of the feet, dozens of other small and often overlooked hints and suggestions. That little book turned out to be a goldmine.

My dad bought me a pair of leather spats. They looked kind of like the canvas leggings WWII soldiers and marines wore but these were only ankle high and on the outside of each there were four or five little loops which contained lead weights. With weights in all the loops, these babies were heavy! I started wearing them when I ran. I wore them around the house, going up and down the stairs, shooting hoops in the driveway and mowing the lawn. I slowly added more and more of the weights and it was working; my speed was improving. I concluded that being a fast runner was not a God-given talent but just the result of hard work and attention to details. That work would pay dividends next season when I went out for football as a sophomore but for now, I'll go back to my freshman year and the excitement associated with Friday-night football.

After our freshman game ended, we showered and dressed, then we went back out to watch the Varsity play.

We weren't the only ones watching. I think ninety percent of Watseka's population came to the games and they were fanatical supporters. I desperately wanted to be one of those guys who were the focus of attention and I was more determined than ever that I would be out there on that field, so I decided that someday, I would be.

My friends and I figured out that we could pick up some easy cash by going back to the field early on Saturday mornings after a home game. We would crawl around under the bleachers looking for loose change that had been dropped during the game; nickels, quarters, dimes, occasionally some actual folding money. It was all there just for the taking. Back then fifty cents or a dollar was a big score; so, there was plenty of incentive to get up early and walk or ride bikes to the field. Yeah, we were high-school kids but we still acted like stupid, grade-school boys, in many ways.

Football season ended in early November. Coach MacKenzie made it clear that unless we were going out for the basketball team, track season starts the Monday after football season ends. We ran through the hallways and up and down the stairs all winter long. These workouts were "optional". I seldom saw Coach there and no one kept track of our attendance but somehow Coach MacKenzie knew who was there working and who wasn't. He always knew. It was uncanny and maybe a little scary. I made sure I never missed a workout and I wore my spats. One of the seniors, a guy everyone called "Cat" noticed them and thought they were a great idea. Cat, as his nickname probably indicated was lightning fast and one of the premier track stars of the entire area. I tried to pick his brain and watched his techniques. We soon became friends and usually did out workouts together. Cat was a sprinter and track was his only sport. He was graceful and lightning fast. When he ran, it seemed like his feet never touched the ground. I studied him and I tried to copy his movements, just as I had done when I'd tried to copy Warren Spahn and Sandy Koufax, when I was learning how to pitch, in baseball. I couldn't match his speed but I bounded up and down those stairs and hallways right along with him. I was looking forward to track season!

The first semester had, as its finale, the Annual Christmas Concert. The Mixed Chorus performed, "The Messiah", and it was spectacular! Our director, Mrs.

Myers, prepared us well. It is a difficult piece of music, with multiple entrances and exits for all the parts; bass, baritone, tenor, alto, and soprano. We hit them all perfectly and on pitch.

In January, after a nice Christmas vacation, it was back to school. I kept my pitching arm in shape by throwing snowballs. Walking to and from school, every street sign, every telephone pole, most of the other kids I saw, and many passing cars became my targets. I made it a point to always carry an extra pair of gloves, so I was always ready. Throwing at moving cars was the best challenge. I had to be far enough away to not get caught, if someone decided to chase me and be effectively hidden so I could not be easily identified. I made a few beautiful, long throws that found their mark and, that was always a huge thrill.

Snowball fights were an everyday occurrence, when the snow was of the right texture and degree of wetness. Sometimes, my friends and I would hustle out of school at the end of the day and get set up across the street. As the rest of the students came out, we pelted them mercilessly with accurate snowball fire. It wasn't long before Mr.

Grant, the Principal at WCHS, was at the door shaking his fist at us and threatening us with lifelong detentions and phone calls to our parents. We thought that we were on firm legal ground since we were neither on school property nor engaging in a school activity, however, we did cease and desist at that point. At least temporarily. We simply moved up and down the blocks near the school, looking for targets of opportunity.

There were basketball games to attend and often they were followed by a school dance in the gym. I was never interested in basketball. Sure, I wanted the Warriors to win but it was more fun watching the cheerleaders, in their short skirts, than watching a bunch of guys running around in shorts. Several of my buddies shared a similar opinion.

The dances became less intimidating. The relationships I enjoyed with my female classmates were casual. I could shuffle around the gym floor with the best of them when a "slow song" was playing. Fast dance songs usually drove me to the sidelines but I had fun. There was no hot romance for me and my buddies and I enjoyed the company of some of the girls, mostly as a group; just a bunch of relaxed, fun-loving kids, who didn't feel the need to pair up as steady dates.

During the week, I continued my hallway workouts, after school, trying to get ready for track season.

Winter finally gave way to Spring and the track team worked out in the sunshine after school. I learned to run the hurdles in grade-school mainly because our coach couldn't find anyone else who was willing to try it. I was determined to make the hurdles my main event on the high-school team. There were two races – the 180-yard low-hurdles and the 110-yard high-hurdles. The "Lows" consisted of eight hurdles spaced twenty yards apart. The "Highs" were ten hurdles spaced ten yards apart. The lows' were 30 inches high, and the highs' were 36 inches high.

I loved running the lows'. I worked hard on the proper technique, trying to clear each hurdle without breaking stride, taking the correct number of steps between each hurdle and being fast. I worked on my "starts", exploding out of the starting blocks at the sound of the starter gun, exactly measuring my stride to reach the first hurdle in such a way that I would have to stretch my lead leg to clear it, then snap the trail leg over, parallel to the hurdle and just grazing the top of it. It was a beautiful race to watch, so rhythmic and graceful. It was even more beautiful to be a competitor in one of the lanes on the track doing it. The lows' became my race. I won the event in my first high-school track meet and as I remember it, breaking the tape stretched across the finish line surprised me and made me flinch a little. The high hurdles were intimidating. Kneeling in the starting blocks and looking down the track, all I could see was a solid barrier of white and black, wooden slats. I never won a race in the highs' but I was able to help the team with a few second and third-place finishes.

Watseka had always been known for its football teams but the track team was damn good! We had several All-State athletes among the upper-classmen. Bruce Sullivan was All-State in absolutely everything! Football, basketball, track; he was even All-State in band and chorus. He was an amazing athlete and later he was an All-American football player at the University of Illinois. We had "Cat" Ellis dancing down the track in the 100 and 200-yard dashes and setting records in the long jump. A senior named Ron, was a short, skinny guy who walked with a slight limp but he could clear a 13-foot-high bar in the pole vault event. Perhaps the athlete I watched the most was a middle-distance runner named Dick Gossett. He was a couple of years older, maybe three, about my size and weight but he had a beautiful, long, powerful running stride, seemingly effortless and fast. I always tried to study the people who could do something better than I could. I wanted to learn how to do what they were able to do. Dick always wore a navy-blue stocking cap on his head, no matter what the weather. It was his mark of distinction, his badge of honor. He offered me encouragement and told me that he thought I was a fine hurdler, for a freshman. Words like that, coming from an upper-classman and a star athlete, really bolstered my confidence.

Many of the meets were competitions between just two schools, Dual Meets. Later in the spring, there were Invitational Meets, involving multiple schools, then County Meets, Conference Meets, Regional and District Meets, and for a select few, who qualified, the State Meet. These were day-long affairs, with lots of down-time between events. We sat around and ate oranges and honey to keep our energy levels up and we made friends with athletes from other schools.

Track was much less stressful than football. The competition was fierce but somehow more subdued. Except for the relay races, track events are individual contests, so, all I had to be concerned with was my own performance. During my high-school career, I never made it to the State Meet. The closest I came was running in the District Meet my sophomore or junior year, I can't remember now which one. I ran the lows' in that meet, against a guy named John Wright. John still holds the State record in the 180-yard low-hurdles and later was an All-American wide receiver at The University of Illinois. I had one of my best times that day but he absolutely smoked me in that race.

The school year comes to an end and it is once again time to concentrate on baseball and working for my father at the Ritz.

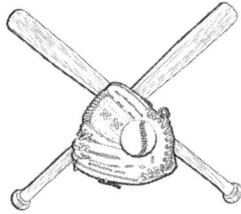

Working at The Ritz

My dad's restaurant was a popular place to meet, eat, drink coffee, and indulge in a huge variety if ice-cream concoctions. Working at the Ritz was my Summer job. Most of the time, I was the soda-jerk. My area of operations was behind the lunch counter. Everything back there was polished stainless steel, polished by me, continuously. A long freezer compartment held at least six flavors of ice-cream; chocolate, vanilla, strawberry, butter-pecan, peppermint, and maybe, English Toffee. There was also lemon, lime, strawberry, and orange sherbets. A heavy-steel, insulated hatch covered each variety for easy access. Above the ice-cream freezer, there was a dizzying array of syrups and toppings; blueberry, blackberry, strawberry, pineapple preserves, plus chocolate, strawberry, butterscotch, and caramel syrups. Next to the ice-cream was a the three-basin sink and drying area.

Along the back wall, behind the counter, was all the glassware; soda glasses, banana-split boats, tall glasses for ice-cream sodas and parfaits, and stainless-steel sundae cups, which were fitted with waxed-paper inserts. Further down, toward the fry-cook area, there were two, big, five-gallon milk dispensers and two huge coffee urns. Everything behind the counter shone brightly, all the time, because it was constantly being polished with damp cheesecloth rags. Cheesecloth. Soft, finely-woven cotton, much like fine gauze. It was ideal for polishing the surfaces back there and after serving customers, polishing the brightwork was the highest priority.

The place was like a laboratory, or maybe a sterile operating room and I was the, "Mad Scientist". There were tall, steel, milkshake cans and a big mixer with four stations for making shakes and malts. I was the master of this craft! My personal favorite was my (should be patented) hot-fudge malt with peppermint ice-cream and a raw egg.

I remember one time when I was working in the afternoon, during the summer. A bus-load of kids stopped in front of the restaurant. Around thirty boys and girls who had been to a baseball game in Chicago, stopped for a snack on their way home. Every one of them wanted a milkshake or a malt. For at least an hour, it was nonstop scooping, pumping, mixing, pouring and cleaning for me.

My friend, "Buzz" was the fry-cook that day and the grill was loaded with hamburger patties, with the deep fryers filled with sizzling french-fries. He was slicing onions and tomatoes, like a surgeon in a combat zone.

Somehow, we filled all the orders and the waitresses scurried back and forth with armloads of plates and glasses. Quite a bit of money found its way into the cash-register that day but Buzz and I were worn out. We worked until closing time. I think it was ten o'clock. We each took a supper break during the shift. He cooked for me and then I cooked for him. That was our usual routine. One time and it might have been the day of the bus load, it was his turn for chow. I made him his usual burger and fries. After he'd finished, I said, "hey Buzz, how about some dessert?".

He said, "sure, I'll take a chocolate sundae!". It is amazing how much a scoop of mashed potatoes looks like a scoop of vanilla ice-cream. Buzz tucked into a beautifully rendered sundae, complete with whipped cream and a cherry on top. Apparently, the chocolate covered spuds were not to his liking. I laughed. He laughed and he vowed to get even.

My dad was the ideal "boss". He was patient, yet demanding. Everything he expected his employees to do, he did himself. Clearing and cleaning the tables, sweeping the floors, serving food, refilling coffee cups, food-prep and cooking. There was nothing he considered too menial for himself to perform and he led from the front and by example. He taught us everything we needed to know to make his business profitable and a fun place to work; taking care of customers, cooking, meal presentation, cleanliness, hustle, and friendliness. Many of my friends and classmates worked at the Ritz from time to time and they all loved the experience. His Naval leadership skills were always in evidence. We didn't mop up spills, we "swabbed the deck". When customers walked in and sat down, we didn't just get busy, we "turned to". We, "commenced ship's work!" All my dad had to do to get our attention was to raise two fingers and rotate them back and forth, the signal to, "turn to". Years later, friends still remember working in, or hanging out, at the place with the blue swimming pool on the ceiling. In the dining area there was an elliptical extension suspended from the ceiling and back lit with soft blue lights. It was a cool place.

DAVID SAMARAS

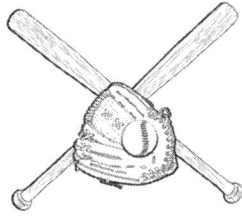

Sophomore Year

Football practice started again in August and as usual, it was the hottest and driest month of the year. The "two-a-day" practices were never easy but this time around I was better prepared. I had added about ten pounds to my formerly skinny frame and I was a few inches taller. Still not a big guy, by football standards but I could run. The previous track season, the weighted spats and the, admittedly sporadic, summer workouts gave me the speed that the coaches noticed. I made the starting lineup on the JV team, as a running back. I played every game that year and I made my share of mistakes. I also made some good plays and worked my tail off to get better during each game and practice. I finally felt like I belonged on a football field. I also suffered my first football injuries that season. The first was a simple sprained ankle. I got tackled by multiple players on a running play and was turned into a pretzel. I limped off the field. The trainer took off my high-top football shoe and sock and taped up the sore ankle. I went back into the game and continued to play. The real pain came after the game, in the locker room, when I had to rip off all that tape. Needless to say, after that, I began shaving my ankles. Later that season I got my first concussion. I took a pitchout from the quarterback and was running parallel to the line of scrimmage. When I made the cut to turn up-field, to gain some yardage, I was met head-on by a linebacker, who probably outweighed me by 30 pounds. He lowered his head, I lowered mine and we collided like a couple of mountain goats. I don't think I lost consciousness but when I started to jog toward the opposing team's huddle, Coach took me out of the game. When I took off my helmet, I saw that it had split and there was a big crack in it.

Coach MacKenzie moved me up to the Varsity for the last few games. Putting on that beautiful maroon and gold uniform, being with the "Big Team" and stepping onto Blake Field on Friday nights with the Varsity was a thrill beyond compare. I played on "Special Teams"; punt coverage and punt returns, kickoff coverage and kickoff returns. I made a few tackles, caught a few punts and had a couple of long kickoff returns. I got to be on the field enough that when we had our annual football banquet at the end of the season, Coach MacKenzie presented me with my first "Varsity Letter"!

The school year was less challenging and a lot more fun. My grades were good. My friends and I continued to have fun in a variety of ways and in January, I reached the magic age of sixteen! I think I was more nervous going to the driver's licensing station than I ever was before or during any athletic competition I had entered. I passed the written, "Rules of the Road" test, then got behind the wheel with an unsmiling (probably former Gestapo Agent) who would evaluate my driving skills and decide my fate. The road test is a blur in my memory but I must have made all the correct turns, squeezed into a parking space and obeyed the posted speed limit, because somehow, I passed! That coveted little paper card that had the words, "State of Illinois Driver's License," at the top, was mine!

No, my parents did not buy me a car. In order to drive somewhere, I had to have an ironclad reason. Parental calculations were made regarding how long it would take me to reach my destination, how much time I would spend there and how much time it would take me to get back home. Permission may or may not be granted to borrow one of the family cars. If it was, I would be given a time to be home and the grace period had precious little margin for error. I did the best I could, to abide by these rules, so, the number of times I could cruise past a friend's house and honk was limited. It didn't matter. I was able to go places wearing my brand-new, varsity-letter jacket and I made sure that as many people as possible saw me!

Becoming a first-time driver during the month of January has certain drawbacks. It was too cold to put the top down on dad's Buick convertible and the streets could be icy and slick. My career as a hot-shot, big-stud driver came to a sudden halt when, while waving to some friends walking down the sidewalk, I lost control of the car and gently slid into another car parked along the side of the street. The damage to both cars was minimal but my ego took a huge hit. Dad was in the car with me at the time, so he already knew that I wasn't trying to show off but he took full advantage of the opportunity to hold an in-depth discussion on winter-time driving hazards and the need for extra caution. I received the message loud and clear.

Just as in the previous year, I was running in the halls after school. My mentor, "Cat" Ellis had graduated the previous May, so, I had to motivate myself to put in quality work. Several of my classmates joined me and we found that running and laughing made for a fun and productive combination. The weather finally started to get warmer and I was able to borrow the car more often. After all, I had lots of important trips to the library to make and I was determined to be the first to be seen riding around town with the top down. Stocking cap, heavy gloves, a wool sweater on under my jacket and heater cranked up full blast! I can't say for sure if I was first but it had to have been a very close contest.

Winter gave way to Spring, and it was track season again. I competed in four events, high hurdles, low hurdles, the half-mile relay, and the mile relay. Running 220 yards in the half-mile relay was fun. The distance isn't much different than the 180 yards in the "lows'". Working on baton exchanges was a lot of fun. Timing and execution were the key elements. The runner carries the baton in his left hand. There is a twenty-yard long area in which the exchange must be made. The timing comes into play when the baton-carrying runner yells, "go" and the next runner in the relay takes off running at full speed and extends his right arm back. The perfect execution takes place when the baton is slapped into the palm of the next runner without either one breaking stride and staying within the twenty-yard exchange area. The exchange is "blind" meaning that the next runner does not look back to receive the baton. As soon as he feels it in his right hand, he immediately transfers it to his left hand and continues down the track. Good exchanges can make the difference between winning and losing the event. When it is done perfectly, it is a beautiful thing to watch and even more beautiful to be a part of.

Running 440 yards in the mile relay was grueling torture. We called the 440 the "guts race". The idea for most of us, at that level of competition, was to sprint all-out for the first 110 yards or so, then try to lengthen your stride and relax, while still carrying the speed for the next

220 yards and then turn on the "after-burners" and sprint the final 110 yards to the exchange or to the finish line. Having enough left for the final 110 yard "stretch kick" is what separated the men from the boys, so to speak. This is where the "guts" came into play. If, by the time you either passed the baton or crossed the finish line, you collapsed in complete exhaustion, you had probably run a good race. It was brutal and I always dreaded it. That was the year I made it to the District Meet and ran against the guy who still holds the State Record in the 180-yard low hurdles. I already told you how that turned out. It was a good season for me and for the track team and I earned my second varsity letter.

My high-school career is half over and I feel a lot different than I did on that first day of class as a freshman. I am having a great time and really looking forward to the next year but first the summer beckons.

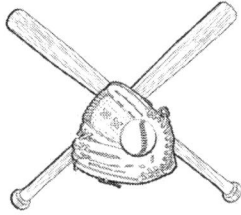

Summer Baseball: The Next Level

As a sixteen-year-old, I was no longer eligible to play in the Babe-Ruth league, so, if I wanted to continue playing baseball, I had to try out for and make the American Legion team. I made the team with ease. I was learning that left-handed pitchers who can throw strikes are prized possessions. Legion baseball is for players 16 to 18 years of age. The competition is a lot tougher. Players are bigger, stronger, and faster and most of them have reached the point where the game of baseball is a serious business to them. My kind of people! We had a good team. Most of the guys were from Watseka but there were a few from some of the nearby smaller towns. We played against teams from all over the state and against some from

Indiana. I am guessing that we won about as many games as we lost that year, so, in terms of being competitive, we were even with the rest of the league.

My two favorite sports, baseball and football are different in so many ways, yet similar in others. Both sports are highly competitive. Both require considerable strength, speed, and finesse. And for me, both were challenging and fun. The differences are what I find most interesting. On the baseball field I had been taught to keep my emotions in check. Coaches continuously preach to, "...control your body language. There must be no open, negative displays. It's okay to get mad, just make sure nobody else knows about it." I've heard coaches say, "if someone looks into our dugout halfway through a game, he shouldn't be able to tell if we are ahead by ten runs or behind by ten." Everything must be positive and upbeat at all times on a baseball field. Successful players learn to do this because the very essence of baseball is "failure". A Hall-of-Fame caliber player is only successful three times out of every ten at bat. Add to this the idea that baseball is more of a marathon than a sprint. The games have no time limit and there are games several times a week during the season. The game must be played with a calm, even-keeled, mental state. Many years ago, when I coached young players, I instituted the "two second rule". This rule states, in part, "...when you strike out, make an error, miss a ball, make an out, or think you got a bad call, it's okay to be upset but only for two seconds. After that, you shake it off, run back to your position or back to the dugout. You put a smile on your face and tell yourself, 'I'll do better next time'." I needed to appear as though I had ice water in my veins. Any kind of negative body language was soundly discouraged and I worked hard to maintain the demeanor that would give nothing away to my opponent. This approach to the game has been taught, stressed, and practiced for decades. All successful players have mastered it, at least to some degree. For a pitcher it is even more important. Being in the center of the diamond, with the ball in his hands, the pitcher is always the center of attention. All his actions are closely watched; by the opposing team, in search of a weakness and by his own teammates, for confidence and leadership. That puts tremendous pressure on the pitcher and I discovered that I absolutely loved that added pressure and responsibility. I never started a game I didn't think I was going to win and I never faced a batter who I thought could get the best of me. My attitude and approach to playing the game were much different than the reality, of course, but that didn't matter, because when I did lose or gave up a big hit, I always knew that there would be another opportunity.

I think one of the things I liked most about football is that showing emotions is encouraged. In football I could get angry and show it. In football, displays of emotion are cultivated and even manufactured to some extent. It was competitive. Who can be the loudest? Who can slam his fist into a locker the hardest? Who can snarl, sputter, and become the most wild-eyed? Getting "fired-up" is part of the game. Players pound on lockers and often on each other, before games, to heighten their emotions. Football is a violent, more physically aggressive sport, where part of the aim is to inflict and to be able to endure pain. I could yell and scream during practices and games. I was always a much better baseball player but playing football was a welcome outlet. Football is more violent, less subtle, more speed and brute strength than finesse. The two sports complement each other in that respect. From my perspective, I loved the differences. Letting emotions burst forth was a welcome change, after the more controlled, emotional discipline baseball required.

Summer baseball came to an end sometime in July and it was time to hang out at the Legion Park swimming pool. Mostly we ogled the tanned, long-legged lifeguards. Many of them were college girls, home for the summer and one was the current Miss Illinois in some beauty pageant! We tried to impress them by making tremendous splashes. "Cannonballs" and "can-openers," off the high-board worked pretty well. We got their attention, maybe an occasional smile and life was good! It was also time to engage in epic water-balloon fights. By this time, several of my classmates had gotten their driver's licenses and had access to a car or a pickup truck. A pickup truck makes for an ideal artillery platform in a water balloon assault. We bought balloons by the hundreds, filled them with water and tied them off. We carefully packed our delicate, jiggly bombs into several plastic laundry baskets. Three or four guys in the back of a pickup with a couple of baskets of water balloons can cut a wide swath of hilarious devastation around town. Legion Park and the nearby streets, during the heat of the summer, constituted a "target-rich-environment". Adults, especially older adults were usually spared. Everyone else we could hit with an accurate throw got drenched. Our water balloon blitz reached its climax and subsequently came to an abrupt halt when I had the bright idea of hauling a couple of baskets of squishy missiles up to the roof of the Ritz. Looking down on Watseka's main business district, from four-stories up, made us feel invincible and invisible. As it turned out, we were neither. We launched our cold, liquid assault on unsuspecting shoppers and many of my dad's customers. He was not amused! I don't recall the exact punishment I earned for these minor indiscretions but the term, "grounded" sticks in my mind. That incident was probably rivaled only, by the infamous gunpowder incident of a few years earlier, in terms of the level of my father's displeasure. I took some serious heat for that but man was it fun.

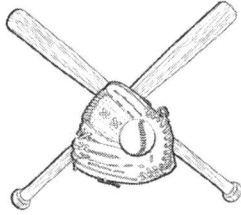

Junior Year

I think the junior year of high-school was the best of all. It was a time when I felt the most comfortable and had the most confidence in myself. As a student, it was the time to start preparing for college but knowing that there was still plenty of time, so, there was really no pressure. There was still going to be one more year to get everything done.

As an athlete, I reached a goal I had been pursuing since that first freshman football practice. I made the starting lineup on the Varsity. I played defensive back that season. I got to know the thrill of hearing my name announced over the P.A. system at the beginning of the game and I got to run onto the field in front of nearly the entire population of Watseka. Just as it is for me in baseball, the same is true of my football memories. I cannot recall the entire experience, or tell you what happened in each game but there are moments I can relive with some clarity. I can remember drawing a bead on a running back during the game against Rantoul. He was a big, strong guy and easily their best player. He was an "air-force brat" from California and his dad had recently been transferred to Chanute Air-Force Base in Rantoul. He tried to get around me but I slammed my head and shoulders into the center of his chest. I hit him so hard I could her the air gushing out of him! We affectionately called hard tackles like that, "snot-bubblers".

I had a long kickoff return when we played Hoopeston for their homecoming game. The best one was when I stepped in front of a wide receiver in the Gibson City game. I intercepted the pass and returned it 40 yards for a touchdown. I remember planning to throw the ball into the air, as I crossed the goal line but I never got the chance. I was tackled in the end zone but it was still a touchdown – my only one as a Varsity player.

I missed our own homecoming game. We were

setting things up for the dance a day or two before the game. Somehow a piano fell over and landed on my foot. Nothing was broken but it swelled up like a balloon and was sore! I watched my teammates, from the sidelines, while standing on a pair of crutches. I was disappointed and all my friends teased the hell out of me but since I was a junior, I knew I would get another chance to play "next year". That, for me, is the reason why junior year was the best. Sure, the seniors were at the "top-of-the-heap" in school and on the athletic fields but for them there would be no next year.

I remember that year as easy and relaxing. Things seemed to "click into place" on the football field that year. The highs I experienced, overshadowed the lows by a wide margin. Practices were still tough and sometimes brutal and the early morning film sessions were still tense and traumatic, especially after a loss the previous Friday night. Sometimes, I was singled out for making a good play and sometimes I had to listen to the projector whir to a stop, rewind a few frames and restart as I watched myself missing a tackle or being out of position on a particular play.

School dances were more fun. Girls began to accept my invitations to dance more frequently but none of them ignited the spark that would transform her from dance partner to girlfriend. My buddies and I continued to act like idiots when the mood struck us. Sneaking into the Sock-Hops by crawling through a window in the boys' restroom was a regular occurrence and saved us the fifty-cents admission fee. One time, we were challenged by a tall, young guy who we didn't recognize. We ignored him, when he told us to go back the way we came and come in through the main entrance like everyone else. It wasn't until later that we found out that he was the new freshman math teacher. Mr. Culbertson didn't find our antics funny but we sure did!

Toward the end of that first semester that "spark" I mentioned earlier, burst into flame. I had never seen her before but there she was, coming out of a classroom and walking toward me. It all happened in a flash. A beautiful face, magnetic and mesmerizing blue eyes, and a shy smile directed at me! The lump in my throat and the sudden inability to breathe, for a moment, provided me with a thrill I had not previously known. Who is she? I had to find out.

I told my friend Buzz about her one day, when I went over to his house to play pool. Buzz's younger sister, Maryann heard our conversation and said, "I know who she is. She's a freshman, like me; she's in girls' and mixed chorus and she lives right across the street. Her name is Linda and she has been talking about you."

Talking about me? A freshman? Chorus? Suddenly my interest in attending choral rehearsals increased tenfold. The next time we had Mixed Chorus practice, I scanned the faces. I spotted her immediately and she was even prettier than the image that was already burned into my brain. As a baseball player, I approached every game with complete confidence and I fully expected to win. This wasn't baseball. I had zero confidence. I had no plan. The term "socially inept" would be a perfect description of me at that time.

I don't remember when it was that I finally worked up the courage to approach her and talk to her and I don't remember what I said to her or what she said to me. Whatever it was, it must have worked out because she seemed interested. It wasn't long before this budding romance hit a couple of snags. Linda's older sister, Kathy was a senior and a member of the Mixed Chorus. She must have casually mentioned the sparkle in her little sister's eyes, to their parents. The edict came down hard and fast. Linda was forbidden to date a boy two years older than she.

The other event which changed things for us and permanently altered our view of the world occurred on November 22, 1963. For me, it was right after lunch. I walked back to school for my American History class. I remember sitting at my desk along with the other students for several minutes. Where is Mr. Dowling? Finally, when he came into the room, he was wringing his hands and had a very strange look on his face. When he spoke, it was almost a whisper. "President Kennedy has been assassinated. He was shot in Dallas and he is dead." He then gathered himself slightly and told us that class and school was dismissed and that we should all go straight home. When I walked in the door, my parents, like the rest of the country were in shock. The TV was on and, we watched hour after hour, as Walter Cronkite relayed all the latest information. It was one of those moments in time that will always be remembered, in vivid detail, by those who experienced it.

The fact that Linda and I were not allowed to date one another became a challenge instead of a deal breaker. We found ways to communicate and to suddenly and subtly, see each other, as if by accident. I spent a lot of time at Buzz's house and played a lot of whiffle ball, baseball catch, and football in his side yard, just hoping to get a glance of his neighbor across the street. We knew each other's class schedules and it became easy to plan casual encounters in the halls between classes. She always let me know when she needed to make a trip to the Post Office or was going to be shopping at one of the stores downtown.

Our (puppy) love affair was more cerebral than it was physical but for both of us it was exciting and as satisfying as we could make it. The fact, that it was forbidden by her parents, just made it that much more enticing. I became good at writing letters and love notes to her. I even tried my hand at poetry. We were studying Shakespeare in English Literature at the time, so, the sonnet became my style of choice.

While most teenagers of my generation could spend hours talking to their girlfriends on the phone, in the evenings and on weekends, we couldn't do that. Her mother would not allow it and she was a woman who absolutely scared the crap out of me. Being told that I cannot do something always provides me with enough incentive to figure out how to do it anyway and Linda and I did just that. The two of us, along with everyone else in our known world, listened to WLS radio out of Chicago all the time. We all had transistor radios and we were inundated with Top-40 rock and roll music continuously. The station sounded a loud tone at the top of each hour. My devious, diabolical, and stunningly brilliant plan was this. At the agreed upon time, usually midnight, I would dial all but the last digit of her telephone number. I would turn the phone dial to the last number and let it go just as the tone on the radio sounded. She would pick up the phone, on her end, at that exact moment and we would be connected, without the phone ringing at her house. It worked! We spent many happy hours talking to each other, teasing, fumbling for words to express our feelings, laughing and exchanging long, deep sighs. There were many times when we got through a day at school without having slept the night before and we still managed to walk on air. Young love! First love! Sweet memories of fleeting moments!

The rest of the school year was kind of a blur. I still ran in the hallways during the winter, went to basketball games and worked at the Ritz but it was those brief moments and long conversations with the auburn-haired, blue-eyed girl that were the highlights of that year. During track season, I had one more fan watching me run my races. I was undoubtedly more distracted than I should have been. Many times, my "warmup" time was spent talking to a pretty girl who seemed to have developed a sudden interest in the sport. I was still competitive when the starter's gun went off and I had someone I was trying to impress. It turned out to be a good season for me.

Summer legion-ball was exceptionally good that year. All the work I had done, especially during the football season, strengthened my legs and my core muscles. My fastball had a little more, "pop", that year. I was still throwing my other pitches for strikes. I was beginning to intimidate batters. I loved that feeling. I loved firing a hard fastball right under the chin of an aggressive hitter just to let him know that the "strike-zone" belonged to me. At the plate, I hit the ball better than I had before. Our team dominated the league and at some of our home games, there was that cute little girl watching me play.

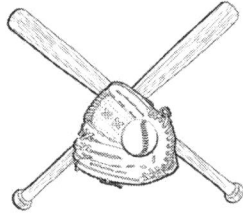

Senior Year and the End of Childhood

That year had a bittersweet quality about it, in some ways. Four years of high-school football was coming to an end. Once the football season started, all of us seniors were silently counting the games we had left. For most of us, it would be the last time we ever played the game. A few of us had the opportunity to play college ball but our numbers were very small and, for me, even though playing in college was exciting and fairly prestigious, the bonds formed on that Watseka Warriors team could not be duplicated. I was still a starter on the defensive team and I think I had a pretty good season. The only game I remember was the last one.

We always played Milford to end our season and we

usually beat them easily. Milford is a town barely ten miles from Watseka. It was quite a bit smaller and not a member of our Athletic Conference. That year, Milford had an outstanding team. They were undefeated when they came to our field and their offence was averaging nearly 40 points per game. They took the field with revenge on their minds and in their hearts. Coach McKenzie's game plan and instructions to us was simple, "we stop them!"

The game drew the biggest crowd I had ever seen on our home field. I think the entire populations of both towns squeezed into creaking bleachers and rimmed the entire field standing four and five-deep. It was to be a battle! We held them to just two field goals, six points, no touchdowns. The defense played their hearts out and I managed to make a couple of good plays in key situations, to stop them. Our offence methodically drove down the field in the fourth quarter, playing an impressive rendition of, "smash-mouth-football", and scored the inevitable touchdown. The extra point made the final score seven to six and a victory in our final game.

The celebration in the locker room was raucous but after it died down, there were a bunch of seniors sitting quietly in front of our lockers. We fingered mud-stained jerseys and held helmets for the last time. Coach McKenzie came around and talked to each one of us individually. I can't remember what he said but I remember that emotions ran high for a few minutes. Sweat wasn't the only thing dripping off some of our faces. We showered, dressed and went out to see our parents and friends. We were seventeen, so, we bounced back fast and it was back to having fun again.

Preparing for the SAT's (Scholastic Aptitude Test), an important college admissions requirement, took up extra study time. I applied to and was accepted by several colleges, including the University of Illinois, Illinois State University, and Trinity College. I also applied to the United States Naval Academy. That was where I really wanted to go. The application process for Navy was much more detailed and demanding than any of the others. It followed a strict progression of hurdles you were required to cross. Once you completed one step, to the satisfaction of a Review Board, you were eligible to move on to the next. The first step was to have an endorsement from either a U.S. Senator or a Congressman. Then there was a multipage application, submission of transcripts and letters of recommendation from teachers and coaches. Next came the Security Clearance protocol. I had to be investigated by the FBI! I still remember old friends of the family from Hoopeston calling my mom and saying, "Carolyn, why is the FBI here asking questions about David?"

The final step in the process was a detailed and all-inclusive, physical exam administered by military personnel. I went to Chanute Air-Force Base in Rantoul for my physical. It took most of the day and I was questioned, palpated, probed, and needle-stuck, like never before. I failed the physical because of my hay-fever. If I had known then what I know now, I would have applied for a waiver. The USNA receives approximately fifteen-thousand applications for admission every year but class size is limited to approximately one thousand. Most applicants are well qualified, so, the physical exam becomes a means for whittling down the hopefuls. Had I applied for the waiver, maybe the Review Board would have said, "hey, this kid really wants this. He played football and ran track for four years. How bad can his hay-fever be? Let's welcome him aboard with an appointment to the Academy."

Back then, I thought that "no" meant "no", so, I decided to go to the University of Illinois. All I had to do was get through the rest of the school year and graduate. That wasn't going to be a problem. I thought the classes were easy. My friend, Buzz was accepted at Notre Dame, and he wanted me to go there with him. My parents said, "no" and that was the end of that discussion.

Linda and I continued our clandestine, albeit limited relationship just as we had before. I enjoyed singing in the chorus more than ever before. When I sang, I was secretly singing to the auburn-haired beauty in the soprano section. In December, we performed the "Messiah" again and I was selected to sing one of the solos. I rehearsed like crazy. My dad was a huge help but when the big moment came, I felt like I was drenched in sweat under my choir robe. Somehow, I got through it. I have no idea how. The feeling of relief when I stepped back to join the rest of the chorus was immense and the brief nod of approval I got, from the director, allowed me to breathe once again.

In January, during my last semester of high-school, two things happened which served to mark the impending

ending of a blissful and memorable childhood. I turned eighteen on my birthday that year. I had to register with the Selective Service Administration and become eligible for military service. I was required to carry my "Draft Card" with me at all times.

The second thing that happened was even more sobering and devastating. My dad announced that he was selling the Ritz. He had bought a hotel and restaurant in Elkhorn, Wisconsin and we were moving there at the end of the school year. That was a bitter pill to swallow. I would have to leave all the friends I had made over the past six years and start over in a new and unfamiliar place. Worse was the realization that the amount of time I could spend with the only real girlfriend I had, was counting down rapidly. I don't think I told her about it until close to the end of the semester. I think I kind of felt my way through that last semester, as if in a fog. A psychologist might say that I was in denial. Maybe so. I tried not to think about it. If being a baseball player had taught me one important thing it was to focus only on the things I can control. I had no control over the decision my parents had made and there was nothing I could do to change that. The only thing over which I had any control was how I would react to the situation. I chose to continue as I had and not let my disappointment show.

Classes continued, the weather warmed, and track season served as a closure to my high-school athletic career. I had earned six Varsity letters. I graduated in the top third of my class and then it was over. Linda's parents finally relented and allowed her to accept my invitation to the Senior Prom. It was a delightful evening of dining in a nice restaurant and dancing together but there was a finality about it known only to me at the time. I wrote Linda a final letter just before we left. It was a long, probably syrupy epistle, in which I promised to be back and that we would always have each other. It didn't happen.

This has been a story about a boy growing up in small towns. It is a collection of memories, mostly accurate and about my love of baseball. The memories fade, friendships dissolve over time, and parents are no longer around. What remains unblemished, bright and pure is baseball. I still love it. I am still involved in it. A happy childhood comes to an end, just like this story.

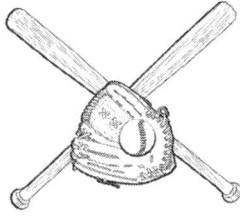

Epilogue

For me, "baseball" is a metaphor for life; life in microcosm, if you will. Every young boy who has ever learned to play the game dreamed of playing in the Major Leagues. Very, very few accomplish that goal and realize that dream but the vast majority (including me) still retain fond memories. The fact that so many of us failed to reach that lofty pinnacle doesn't tarnish the experience of having played the game and having worked so hard in pursuit of perfection. The thrill, the satisfaction, and the beautiful memories came from the journey not the attainment of the goal. That is the message I wanted to convey to those young high-school players. To savor every moment of the struggle, to embrace everything associated with it. Just as in baseball, life is a journey, often with an unknown destination. The ups and downs, the good the bad, the pain and the joy, the laughter and the tears. None of these things can be avoided and all can provide valuable lessons, building memories that can sometimes be recalled, in order to help those behind us on the same journey. A career in baseball, a single season, or sometimes even a single game can give a player an opportunity to experience, at least in a small way, much of what life has to offer. Baseball encompasses perhaps the most ancient of confrontations, a man with a stick against a man with a rock. This, in my opinion, is the essence of baseball. A man standing in the center of the field holding a ball is engaged in a one-on-one battle, with a man with a bat standing at home plate. Each is determined to defeat the other either by applying brute strength, or through the use of stealth and guile. The confrontation between pitcher and batter is non-lethal combat at its very best, with the challenge possibly including strategy, the use of subterfuge and deception. Each maneuver is designed to set up the "kill", the pitch that will cause the batter to make an out. They are two chess masters wearing baseball uniforms.

Someone wins!

Someone loses!

Then the process begins all over again!

How can anyone not love it!

DAVID SAMARAS

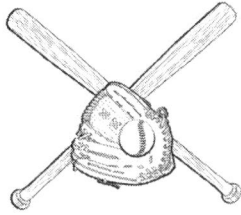

About the Author:

David Samaras is a retired E.P.A scientist.

He played baseball for 19 years and has coached for an additional 17 years.

He is a U.S. Navy veteran.

He and his wife, Mary-Lee reside in Springfield, Illinois, with their four beautiful, black kitties.

Made in the USA
Columbia, SC
21 September 2020